B is for Bitcoin

The Essential Guide to All Things Bitcoin

By Daz Bea & Seb Bunney

TABLE OF CONTENTS

Acknowledgments

No words describe how much Daz and myself (Seb) appreciate the
support and encouragement we received while turning this book from
an idea into a reality.

First, we want to thank the Bitcoin community and the countless
individuals who reached out and offered their time to read over the
first draft and give feedback.

Second, we want to thank Keysa and Gary for their numerous hours
scouring the manuscript and giving their input, feedback and revisions.

And lastly, we want to thank the rest of the Looking Glass team for the
time and effort they've dedicated to bringing this platform to life.

Thank you, everyone!

And on a personal note, I want to thank my wife Carissa and boys Archer and Fletcher and recognize the family time sacrificed for me to pursue these projects.

I truly believe in the message we are trying to spread, and this would not have been possible without your support.

Love Daz (Dad)

Introduction

So, you want to learn about Bitcoin? Well, you've picked up the right book!

One of the long-standing tenets of bitcoiners worldwide is "don't trust, verify."

It can be easy to jump on board the rocketship that is Bitcoin, whether through purchasing, mining or simply involving yourself in the community, without truly understanding what it is.

We believe Bitcoin is arguably the most remarkable technological advancement in history. But don't take our word for it. We want you to verify for yourself and come to your own conclusion.

For this reason, we have written this book, an in-depth exploration of the ins and outs of Bitcoin.

And in true LookingGlass-style, we have taken thousands of hours of research, stripped out the technical jargon, and distilled down the key concepts to give you a thorough understanding of this unique, nascent, paradigm-shifting monetary asset.

We will cover everything from:
- Who is Satoshi Nakamoto, and what is the white paper?
- How does Bitcoin actually work?
- What is the role of the miners, nodes and network participants?
- What options do I have for purchasing and securely storing my Bitcoin?

...all to significantly increase your understanding of this nascent technology.

That may sound a little dry, but we promise to keep it fun, educational and definitely… interesting.

Enough rambling. Let's crack on…

Side note: If you want to understand how bitcoin fits into the larger financial world, we highly recommend you head over to our Foundation's course, "Debt, Inflation and the Bigger Picture," which can be found on our website:

www.lookingglasseducation.com

That is if you haven't already.

CHAPTER 1

The Origins of Bitcoin

"I think the internet is going to be one of the major forces for reducing the role of government. The one thing that's missing but that will soon be developed, is a reliable e-cash." - Milton Friedman in 1999

SECTION 1

The Legend of Satoshi Nakamoto

Key Questions Answered:
Who is Satoshi Nakamoto?
What do we know about Satoshi Nakamoto?
Why did Satoshi create Bitcoin?

Bitcoin wouldn't exist if it weren't for the shadowy faceless super-coder[1], the myth, the legend, Satoshi Nakamoto. We, therefore, felt that there is no better place to start this book than with a deep dive into the mysterious developer behind Bitcoin.

What's more, understanding the origins of Bitcoin helps us gain insight into the "Why" surrounding Bitcoin and helps set the stage for a deeper, more holistic understanding of Bitcoin.

And so, without further ado, let's dive in.

Who is Satoshi Nakamoto?

Honestly, we have no idea who Satoshi Nakamoto is. There is much speculation on who people believe him to be. Some have publicly come forth, claiming that they are, in fact, this mystical figure. But, to this day, no one has been able to prove the identity of the mysterious Satoshi Nakamoto.

Side Note: Due to the limited information available, we must embrace the fact that we are in the dark about whether Satoshi is a guy, a girl, a group of people, or even an organization. With that said, we will refer to Satoshi as a male throughout this book for clarity and consistency, based solely on the fact that the name "Satoshi" has a male connotation in Japanese.

What do we know about Satoshi Nakamoto?

Satoshi first appeared out of the dark shadows of the internet in October 2008 when he sent a nine-page paper[2] titled: "Bitcoin: A Peer-to-Peer Electronic Cash System" to the cypherpunk mailing list[3].

"The Cypherpunks mailing list was… a very active forum with technical discussion ranging over mathematics, cryptography, computer science, political and philosophical discussion, personal arguments and attacks, etc., with some spam thrown in."

Dr. Adam Back, one of the most active contributors and creator of an early e-cash version (Hashcash), explains the introduction of Satoshi here[4].

These cypherpunks were the perfect audience for Satoshi to propose his ideas. They were advocates for cryptography and for the use of privacy-enhancing technology as a means of social and political change. Initially, the mailing list members dismissed the idea, believing it to be just another one of many attempts[5] at a digital form of payment, i.e. B-Money, Bit Gold, and Hashcash, to name a few.

In the words of Satoshi:

"A lot of people automatically dismiss e-currency as a lost cause because of all the companies that failed since the 1990?s. I hope it's obvious it was only the centrally controlled nature of those systems that doomed them. I think this is the first time we're trying a decentralized, non-trust-based system."

Eventually, however, Bitcoin sparked enough interest for one of the cypherpunks to reach out, a guy by the name of Hal Finney. Hal was well-known in the cryptography space due to his deep knowledge base, exceptional coding ability and connections within the community. Satoshi and Hal's relationship quickly grew to the point where Hal would be the first developer to work on Bitcoin alongside Satoshi. Satoshi would focus on updates while Hal assisted with bug fixes. After this, Bitcoin started gaining momentum, triggering more individuals to reach out and offer their assistance to the project. Then, just over two years after releasing the Bitcoin White Paper, Satoshi disappeared.

Fun fact: Hal was the first person to ever receive a bitcoin transaction. On January 12, 2009, Satoshi sent him ten bitcoin.

As far as we know, Satoshi's last message[6] was an email to a fellow developer on April 23, 2011, where he said, *"I've moved on to other things."* Since then, there has been the occasional interaction under the name Satoshi. However, every interaction has been shrouded in doubt, lacking evidence of legitimacy.

One example was a message by an account claiming to be Satoshi declaring:

"I am not Dorian Nakamoto."

This was posted on the p2pfoundation.ning.com[7] forum on March 7, 2014, after a man named Dorian Prentice Satoshi Nakamoto[8] was gaining unwanted publicity from people purporting that he was indeed the real Satoshi. It is believed that Dorian Prentice Satoshi Nakamoto is not the real Satoshi, nor is the account forum posting from March 2014.

As it stands, the consensus amongst the community deems the last official communication from Satoshi to be the message relayed on April 23, 2011.

Why did Satoshi disappear?

We may never know for sure, and so at the moment, all we can do is speculate. Some of the more popular theories are:
- He might have felt his job was done. He had created this new form of internet money and handed it over to the community.
- Satoshi may have been nervous about the attention Bitcoin was getting. In December 2010[9], WikiLeaks was banned from using traditional payment methods (e.g. Paypal, Visa, Mastercard). With no way of obtaining funding, they decided to use Bitcoin. With Bitcoin being only one year old, Satoshi felt this was not the attention Bitcoin needed, *"It would have been nice to get this attention in any other context. WikiLeaks has kicked the hornet's nest, and the swarm is headed towards us,"* he wrote. Considering that it is a criminal offence[10] to create a currency in the US, tied with the fact that Bitcoin was gaining significant adoption, it may have

instilled fear and caused him to move on.
- He might have switched gears to focus on another project, which was the essence of what he wrote on April 23, 2011, in his last email.
- He may have passed away.

Although alluring, piecing together the puzzle of the identity of this mysterious figure doesn't provide us with much information. Therefore, let's shift focus and look at the "why" surrounding Bitcoin's creation.

Why did Satoshi create Bitcoin?

Although we don't have much to go on when answering "who is Satoshi?" when it comes to the question of "why?" we have much more information. Luckily, Satoshi was quite vocal online in the early days of Bitcoin. Through his interactions, we can better understand why he created this magical internet money.

Bitcoin emerged out of the turmoil of the 2008 Global Financial Crisis as distrust grew around banks, their role in the financial system and the role of central banks and governments. We can see from Satoshi's communication that he had cynicism toward the traditional monetary and banking system. This can be seen in the first-ever Bitcoin block, known as the genesis block, where he posted a message which said:

"The Times 03/Jan/2009 Chancellor on brink of second bailout for banks" - Satoshi Nakamoto, Genesis Block

This quote references a Times newspaper article[11] titled "Chancellor on brink of second bailout for banks." In the article, the author highlighted that *"the (British) Chancellor will decide within weeks whether to pump billions more into the economy,"* effectively encouraging banks to engage in risky behaviour, with little consequence to them. This behaviour sent a clear message to the public that fiscal irresponsibility would be *"socialized."* In other words, losses would be shared amongst currency holders rather than the banks taking responsibility for their actions.

Additionally, we know from his more recent messages that Satoshi disagreed with how our current monetary system functioned:

"The root problem with conventional currency is all the trust that's required to make it work. The central bank must be trusted not to debase the currency, but the history of fiat currencies is full of breaches of that trust." - Satoshi Nakamoto

When we combine what we know about Satoshi, a clear picture emerges:

1. Satoshi was part of the cypherpunk mailing list.
2. This group focused on privacy-enhancing technology as a means of social and political change, and various members had previously proposed and tried to implement digital currencies.
3. He proposed a form of electronic cash that does not rely on trusted third parties.
4. He felt it was important to attach the message "Chancellor on brink of second bailout for banks" in the first Bitcoin block.
5. He was vocal about his views on the problems with conventional currency.

Satoshi understood the drawbacks and issues with conventional currency. He, therefore, felt that these issues were big enough for him to focus on proposing another option: A digital peer-to-peer (p2p) cash system that did not require trusted third parties. This would be a currency for the people, by the people, controlled by math. A currency that was not beholden to a centralized authority.

Fun fact: Satoshi accumulated a large amount of bitcoin through mining in the early days of Bitcoin. If someone wanted to prove that they are indeed Satoshi, they could simply move some of this bitcoin. To this day, no one has ever moved any of Satoshi's bitcoin, and if they did move, we would know, as every transaction is public and transparent, but more on that later...

To summarize, we know that Satoshi played a pivotal role in making digital cash a reality by bringing Bitcoin to life with the help of the community. However, there is still much more that we don't know. This begs the question, does it really matter? If Satoshi turned up today, would it change anything?

Keep these questions in the back of your mind as we continue exploring this revolutionary technology and monetary asset.

SECTION 2

Clarity

Key Questions Answered:
What is the difference between Bitcoin and bitcoin?
What are these things called Satoshis?
How many other ways is bitcoin expressed?

Digitally native cash created by a mysterious shadowy figure may be a new concept for most. Moreover, you may come across unfamiliar terms and phrases as you interact with the community. We, therefore, feel it is important to set the stage and clarify some terminology. That way, as you interact with Bitcoiners, you'll understand what on earth they are talking about.

What is the difference between Bitcoin and bitcoin?

You may have noticed that sometimes Bitcoin is spelt with a lowercase "b" and sometimes with an uppercase "B." This is no mistake. Each variation represents something unique. Let's start with the lowercase bitcoin:

bitcoin - "b"
When spelt with a lowercase "b," we are referring to the asset. The asset is the unit of currency for the Bitcoin network (explained below). It is the asset which holds value and can be exchanged between people. For example, if we were to send someone 0.001 bitcoin, they would be receiving bitcoin, the asset.

However, the asset is useless without a network that allows us to send and receive this asset.

This brings us to Bitcoin the network:

Bitcoin - "B"
Bitcoin, spelled with an uppercase "B," refers to the Bitcoin network. It is through the network that the asset is both created and moved. Without the network, we would have no way of sending bitcoin, the asset, to one another.

If this sounds confusing, here is an example:

In the traditional monetary system, we have the wire network and the US Dollar. If we wanted to send a larger sum of money from our bank account to a friend's bank account, we would use the wire network. You can liken this to uppercase Bitcoin.

However, the wire network only facilitates the transfer. It does not store the value. That value is stored in the asset, which in this case is the US Dollar.

Here are a couple of scenarios for each:

- Looking Glass Education aims to educate individuals as to the power of Bitcoin - **The network**
- I'd like to send Hillary 0.0001 bitcoin - **The asset**
- Did Satoshi Nakamoto come up with the idea for Bitcoin? - **The network**
- I have used bitcoin as a savings vehicle for a few years now - **The asset**

What are these things called satoshis?

Within the Bitcoin community, you will regularly hear people referring to satoshis, or sats for short, as an alternate reference to bitcoin. Simply put, a satoshi is the smallest denomination of a bitcoin, similar to how cents make up a dollar, or a penny is a fraction of a pound.

At today's price (~July 2022), bitcoin is trading around $20,000 US dollars. People, therefore, incorrectly believe that to buy bitcoin, they need to spend $20,000. The truth is we can easily purchase a fraction of a bitcoin. Even as little as 0.00000001 bitcoin, otherwise known as one satoshi. That is currently $0.0002.

Each whole bitcoin is made up of 100,000,000 satoshis. To convert between them, take the amount of bitcoin and multiply it by 100,000,000. The result is the amount in satoshis (sats). For example:
- 0.004 bitcoin = 400,000 sats
- 0.000965 bitcoin = 96,500 sats
- 1.38 bitcoin = 138,000,000 sats

With this new understanding, the next time you hear someone talking about sats, you will be up-to-date and in-the-know!

How many other ways is bitcoin expressed?

As Bitcoin has no central controlling entity or governing body pushing a marketing plan, no one is dictating how Bitcoin should be portrayed publicly. With that being the case, you'll encounter a few different Bitcoin abbreviations. Let's focus on two of the primary abbreviations for bitcoin.

"BTC" is the abbreviation/ticker symbol that has been adopted most widely. This originated in the early days of Bitcoin and is regularly used today. However, "XBT" is another that you'll come across. It is used mainly on exchanges to reflect Bitcoin's growing legitimacy as an international currency.

The characters "XBT" come from the International Standards Organization (ISO), which maintains a list of internationally recognized currencies. XBT is to bitcoin as USD is to the United States Dollar, CAD to the Canadian Dollar, MXN to the Mexican Peso etc.

What's interesting to note is that similar to gold (XAU), bitcoin (XBT) has an "X" leading the abbreviation. This is not by chance. If a currency is not associated with a particular country, ISO states that it should begin with an "X," hence "XBT."

Lastly, you may have seen the Bitcoin logo expressed as ₿. This is no different from the dollar symbol ($), or the Great British Pound symbol (£). In terms of usage, the symbol proceeds the quantity of bitcoin, i.e. 0.001 bitcoin = ₿0.001 = 100,000 sats. There is also a symbol for sats. That said, this is still gaining in popularity amongst the community, but it remains to be seen if it will be widely adopted and accepted.

Two bitcoin or two bitcoins? - Plurals

Do you say bitcoin or bitcoins when talking about more than one bitcoin? While Satoshi used "bitcoins" to denote the plural, over time, "bitcoin" (with no "s") has become the standard. You will, however, still find some old-timers in the space refer to them in their plural form, "bitcoins." There is no right or wrong answer.

On the other hand, satoshis/sats are usually referred to in the singular and plural forms. One satoshi, two satoshis, one sat, two sats, for example.

Section Summary

With Bitcoin becoming the globally recognized asset that it is, there are many variations to how it is portrayed. One that often creates confusion is the difference between bitcoin, the asset, and Bitcoin, the network. An easy way to remember this is:

The network (Bitcoin) transfers value from A to B.
The asset (bitcoin) is the value that moves from A to B.

In an attempt to simulate the real world, throughout this book, we will frequently refer to the network and the asset. Additionally, we will use satoshis, sats, and the BTC symbol interchangeably and bitcoin (with no 's') when referring to multiples of bitcoin.

There is no better time than the present to build this knowledge into your vocabulary.

To summarize:

1. Uppercase Bitcoin refers to the network.
2. Lowercase bitcoin refers to the asset.
3. A satoshi, or sat for short, is the smallest denomination of a bitcoin and is equal to 0.00000001 bitcoin, or 10^8 for the math nerds.
4. BTC and XBT are both commonly used abbreviations for bitcoin.
5. The currency symbol for bitcoin is ₿.
6. Bitcoin and bitcoins are used interchangeably for multiples of bitcoin, but it is more common to see bitcoin (no "s"). Satoshis and sats are used in singular and plural forms.

SECTION 3

Bitcoin's Inception

Key Questions Answered:
What is the Bitcoin White Paper?
What is the Byzantine Generals' Problem?
What hurdles did bitcoin face?

With a clear understanding of bitcoin, the asset, Bitcoin, the network, and a patchy understanding of Satoshi, let's now direct our attention to Bitcoin's origin and how this magic internet money first came into existence.

What is the Bitcoin White Paper?

The word 'Bitcoin' was first used publicly on the 31st of October 2008, when Satoshi Nakamoto released what is known today as the Bitcoin White Paper. This is the document which proposed the new peer-to-peer (P2P) electronic cash system.

This doesn't sound too wild until you realize that peer-to-peer means NO intermediaries and NO third parties. This is a lot harder to achieve than it sounds! Before the introduction of Bitcoin, every form of electronic money required intermediaries and trusted third parties.

Previously, we introduced:

bitcoin, the asset– the thing we purchase that's accessible from our wallet;

and

Bitcoin, the network– the rails which facilitate the trade of bitcoin-the-asset. It is the network that allows individuals to send, verify and secure transactions.

When we look at our current monetary system through this same lens of 'the asset' and 'the network,' we realize that we have to trust and rely on third parties and intermediaries in both situations. For instance:

The Asset
The fiat currencies we use as a store of value (E.g. US dollar, euro, yen, franc, pound sterling, etc.).

Fun fact: 'Fiat' literally means 'by decree' or forced to be used with implied threats for non-compliance.

Central Banks oversee Monetary Policy – Monetary Policy is the management of interest rates and the total supply of money in circulation. If the central bank decides to lower interest rates or increase the total money supply, new money suddenly enters the economy, diluting the value of any existing currency in circulation, reducing its purchasing power and contributing to inflation. The exact quantity of most major existing fiat currencies is unknown, even by those that produce them.

Governments oversee Fiscal Policy – Fiscal Policy deals with taxation and government spending. Suppose the government decides to stimulate the economy through lower taxation and stimulus cheques. The population will have more disposable income, which means greater spending which drives up prices (inflation), lowering our purchasing power over time.

We, the people, are at the whims of these decision-makers. We have to trust that our government and the (unelected) central bankers have our best interests at heart regarding monetary and fiscal policy. Otherwise, their decisions can negatively impact our currency's purchasing power and, thereby, our quality of life. Unfortunately, history has shown us that there have been many examples of breaches of this trust.

The Network
The rails that allow us to transact with one another.

When purchasing a coffee using our credit card, there are four or more different intermediaries - First, there is the institution that the coffee shop banks with. Secondly, there are the networks which allow the banks to communicate with one another. Then, there is the association that facilitates the transaction (Visa, Mastercard, Discover etc.). And finally, there is our banking institution.

When sending a wire transfer, we touch four or more third parties - First, we have to provide our bank with the recipient's bank details. Then, as our bank most likely doesn't have direct communication with the recipient's bank, using the SWIFT (Society for Worldwide Interbank Financial Telecommunications) network, the wire information is sent through a correspondent or intermediary bank. Finally, these banks reach out to the recipient's bank to finalize the transaction.

Regulatory bodies oversee various arms of the financial rails that we use day-to-day - For example, suppose our political views oppose those regulating the monetary networks or any part of that intermediary process; our transactions can be blocked, assets seized, and we may be locked out of the financial system entirely.

Does this sound scary or unlikely? This happened in early 2022 when individuals donated to the trucker rally in Canada, and Prime Minister Trudeau had some of these individuals' bank accounts frozen by his decree. Regardless of your views on that particular matter, the fact that people's assets were seized due to their differing views might give you pause for concern.

As is now evident, we must rely on multiple intermediaries and third parties in every transaction within the fiat system, hoping they meet our needs and continue to operate and fulfil our transactions. In the words of Satoshi:

> *"Banks must be trusted to hold our money and transfer it electronically, but they lend it out in waves of credit bubbles with barely a fraction in reserve. We have to trust them with our privacy, trust them not to let identity thieves drain our accounts."*

Outside of the physical, peer-to-peer transfer of cash, we previously had no way of transacting with one another without using trusted third parties. That may seem like a non-issue. However, what happens when a trusted third party doesn't have our best interest at heart, provides unfavourable terms, takes advantage of its users, or devalues the currency for its own benefit?

It should now be clear that we unwittingly place an immense amount of trust in third parties. It is reasonable to conclude that it is due to this potentially dangerous reliance on trust that Bitcoin was born. Satoshi wanted to create a trustless means of transacting that removes reliance on third parties or knowledge of the counterparty in an exchange.

That brings us to the question, how is it possible to create a monetary system that allows individuals to transact with one another without needing to trust third parties?

The Byzantine Generals' Problem

For Bitcoin to offer a viable solution to that question, Satoshi would have to overcome an age-old conundrum known as the Byzantine Generals Problem. Prior to the Bitcoin White Paper, this was a problem thought to be unsolvable.

How can we send a message without the need for trust or a third party?

Or, in the case of Bitcoin, **how can we send or receive bitcoin without this need for trust?**

This is going to get a little philosophical for a moment, so please bear with us. We trust it will be worth it.

The year is 2000 BC. Imagine there is an enemy city surrounded by two armies, one on each side of the city. Both armies need to attack simultaneously to conquer the city, as it is fortified enough to defend itself against either one of the armies, but not both. If they don't attack simultaneously, the city will obliterate one or both armies.

With this in mind, the generals of each army must agree on an exact time to attack to ensure they do so simultaneously. Because of the landscape, the only way to communicate is by sending a messenger back and forth through the enemy city (unfortunately, cell phones aren't invented yet).

The conversation goes something like this. General One sends the message, "Yo, General Two, how does an attack at sunrise on Saturday sound?" The messenger sneaks through the city, delivering the message. General Two responds, "Dang, Saturday doesn't work. We have a full-moon party the night before. What about sunrise on Sunday?" General Two's messenger then quietly runs through the city to deliver the message to General One. This goes back and forth until a decision is made.

This all sounds fine and dandy until we realize that the messenger could be captured in the city and replaced with a conspirator messenger, someone who intentionally deceives the other general, causing one army to attack at the wrong time.

We now face a problem. There is no way to check if a message received is authentic. **How can we create a "trustless" system that ensures victory for the attacking armies?**

This is known as the Byzantine General's Problem.

Amazingly, Satoshi's Bitcoin White Paper solved it! He devised a way to build a peer-to-peer, trustless form of electronic money so that we don't have to rely on trusted third parties, i.e. little messengers running through enemy cities, Visa, Mastercard, banks, governments or other actors. With this in mind, let's look at the hurdles bitcoin faces in solving this trust issue.

The hurdles

For Bitcoin to achieve its lofty goal of becoming a peer-to-peer electronic cash system, it had to overcome some significant hurdles. It had to find a way of removing this trust in third parties. The challenge, each of these trusted third parties served a purpose in the fiat system. They set the rules, verified and settled transactions and prevented the double-spending of money.

Let's explore these:

Rules

From an asset perspective, decisions must be made, such as:

- How much currency should there be in circulation?
- What is the supply schedule?
- How divisible/what denominations should there be?

Currently, these decisions are made by the central banks.

From the network perspective, third parties, such as banks, Visa, Mastercard etc., decide who can and can't transact, what information is needed to transact and transaction costs.

Transaction Verification + Settlement

Each third party in a transaction plays a role in facilitating the exchange. They see to it that every initiated transaction meets the necessary requirements, which allows the transaction to be completed, also known as transaction settlement. Combined, these third parties ensure the transaction network is functionally operational and running smoothly.

Double-spend Problem

Before Bitcoin came to be, digital scarcity did not exist. If we took out our phones to take a picture of a sunset, initially, there would only be one of these pictures in existence. However, we could easily copy and paste that sunset picture as many times as we like and send it to many recipients, eliminating any notion of scarcity.

With this in mind, what is to stop someone from spending their bitcoin, only to have copied their bitcoin's digital information before sending it (just like copying the sunset picture), and spending the bitcoin for a second time? This is known as the double-spend problem. These network third parties, such as Visa and Mastercard, monitor all transactions, ensuring that money is correctly debited from our account and credited to the recipient's account. That way, no one can double spend. They are the overlords of the ledger.

You're now probably wondering, if we remove trusted third parties and intermediaries:
1. Who sets the rules?
2. Who verifies and settles transactions?
3. And how do we ensure money can't be double-spent?

By the end of this book, you will be able to answer how Bitcoin overcame each of these hurdles. Additionally, you will have a deeper understanding of how bitcoin works and everything involved in making this mystical internet money operational.

For further resources, we highly recommend:
"Bitcoin: A Peer-to-Peer Electronic Cash System" - Satoshi Nakamoto

SECTION 4

Bitcoin Overview

Key Questions Answered:
Who are the participants in the Bitcoin ecosystem?
What is the Bitcoin protocol?
What technology underpins Bitcoin?

Alright!! With some of the history behind Bitcoin's origins out of the way, it's time to tear the lid off this and get our hands dirty.

If you're wondering, "what the hell is Bitcoin?" Or "how does it work?" You're in luck, as we are about to find out.

The concepts covered in this section deserve elaboration. So don't be too concerned if the ideas are foreign or ill-defined. We will introduce them here so you can start to piece together the jigsaw puzzle that is Bitcoin. Then throughout the following chapters, we will explore the nitty-gritty details.

Topics surrounding Bitcoin can be vast and complex, from computer science or philosophical debates to how a sound money standard can benefit humanity. However, from a functionality point-of-view, Bitcoin can be distilled down into a few key participants, rules and technologies:

The Participants
- Nodes
- Miners
- Developers
- Community

The Protocol (The Rules)
- Fixed Hard-Cap Supply
- Block Reward & The Halving Cycle
- Block Time & The Difficulty Adjustment

The Technology
- Blockchain
- Distributed Ledger
- Public/Private Key Cryptography

Let's explore each of these, starting with the participants.

The Participants

Nodes
Nodes can be thought of as computers which monitor every Bitcoin transaction. They ensure everyone is playing by the rules and that every transaction meets the requirements set forth through consensus.

Additionally, as Bitcoin is decentralized (there is no reliance on a central authority), the nodes, through consensus, decide what new features and changes to the rules are implemented.

Miners

After a transaction is initiated, but before it is completed, there is no certainty that the transaction will settle– just like one has pending and processed transactions on one's credit card statement. Therefore, the miners' role is to organize and commit these transactions to the permanent record of transactions in the blockchain.

Like a node, a miner is simply a computer, but instead of monitoring transactions, the miners process the transactions.

Bitcoin wouldn't exist without the miners, and the nodes wouldn't have any transactions to monitor.

Developers

The developers are a diverse group of people consisting of highly skilled programmers and digital authors, all working to maintain the network and improve security, privacy, scalability and user experience. They fix any issues and bugs and propose new features that will help keep Bitcoin robust, up-to-date and secure from malicious attacks.

Community

The community is what brings Bitcoin to life and gives it value. They use the network and transact back and forth, incentivizing the nodes, miners and developers to continue working on Bitcoin. As an increasing number of people like you learn about Bitcoin, the community grows, and so does the value of the Bitcoin network.

As should be evident, each and every player plays an integral role in bringing Bitcoin to life.

To summarize the players:
- Nodes are standard computers that set and enforce the rules
- Miners are specialized computers that verify transactions

- Developers are people that keep the software up-to-date and propose upgrades
- The community, everyone enamoured by Bitcoin, is what gives life and value to this ecosystem

The Protocol (The Rules)

A protocol is simply a procedure or system of rules which govern the way something functions. For example, if one was to meet a monarch of a country, there are said to be protocols[12] (rules) in place which need to be followed to show appropriate respect. Similarly, in computing, there are many protocols which make the internet work, which we don't often see and take for granted. These include HTTP (web), SMTP (email), TCP/IP (networking) and now Bitcoin (money).

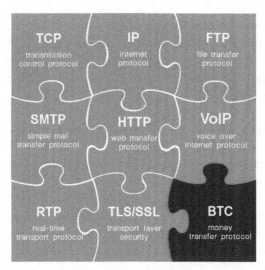

Figure 1.31: The Building Blocks of the Internet[13]

Therefore, when we say the Bitcoin protocol, it's a technical way of saying the rules that make Bitcoin what it is.

With this in mind, let's look at some of the fundamental rules of Bitcoin.

Fixed Hard-Cap Supply

Arguably, the most critical element of what makes Bitcoin a sound monetary good is that there will only ever be a maximum of 21 million bitcoin. This is known as the fixed hard-cap supply.

If you own 0.1 of 21 million bitcoin today, you can be confident that you'll still own 0.1 of 21 million bitcoin in ten years. This is unlike any other currency where the issuance and supply are unknown and at the whim[14] of governments and bankers, removing any attribute of scarcity.

Block Reward & The Halving Cycle

The Block Reward is how new bitcoin is birthed and introduced into the world. When miners solve/mine a block (thereby committing it to the permanent blockchain), they are rewarded for their efforts. This reward consists of:

- The **block subsidy**, which is new, virgin bitcoin of a specified amount (more on that below).
- The **transaction fees** paid by users to have their transactions included in the block.

An important detail is that if miners were rewarded the same amount of bitcoin every time a new block was discovered, there would be no cap on how much bitcoin could enter circulation.

This is where the Halving Cycle comes in.

Every 210,000 blocks (roughly four years), bitcoin has a halving event that is programmed into the base protocol. At this point, the bitcoin block subsidy that miners receive for verifying transactions is halved.

Pre-programmed into Bitcoin's code is a total of 32 of these halving events, spanning roughly 128 years. That means, by 2140, all 21 million bitcoin will have been mined, which is why Bitcoin is said to have a hard-capped supply.

Block Time & The Difficulty Adjustment
Since the inception of Bitcoin in 2009, a new block has been mined on average every ten minutes. This is not by chance. Satoshi designed it this way to ensure a predictable issuance rate for new bitcoin.

The protocol targets this block time of ten minutes through a feature known as the "difficulty adjustment." By fixing the supply of bitcoin entering the market, you remove the potential for unexpected devaluation from dilution.

Every 2,016 blocks (around two weeks), the protocol assesses how quickly miners verify transactions and create blocks. It then adjusts the difficulty of mining accordingly. This was one of Satoshi's genius solutions to help protect the bitcoin issuance from outrunning itself as more advanced computers are developed.

These are the fundamental rules that give bitcoin scarcity, making it desirable. The nodes enforce these rules, ensuring every miner and all transactions abide by them. On every Bitcoin node, a copy of these rules is written into its software.

The Technology

The Blockchain
The blockchain is quite literally how it sounds. A chain of blocks.

Blocks of data, one after the other, linked together to form a chain.

Think of these blocks as little containers that store information, such as transactions. Through this data, we can determine how many bitcoin are in existence, who owns what, and who has sent what to whom.

The first block, known as the Genesis block, was mined by Satoshi on January 3rd, 2009. Since then, a new block containing the most recent transactions has been created and appended to the blockchain roughly every ten minutes. Every one of these new blocks has been checked to be correct by the thousands of nodes enforcing the rules.

Distributed Ledger

As mentioned above, the blockchain contains lots of information. This information makes up what is known as the Bitcoin ledger. It contains a record of who owns what bitcoin and the transaction history of everyone who has ever transacted using bitcoin. All bitcoin transactions are inherently pseudonymous, with transactions being identified by numbers rather than names.

The distributed part of the "distributed ledger" comes from the fact that this information is not centralized. Instead, a copy of this ledger is stored on every node within the Bitcoin network. That way, we never have to rely on trusted third parties or intermediaries to tell us who owns what, as we have a globally distributed record of this information that can easily be accessed by anyone who wishes to do so.

Private/Public Key Cryptography

It is through cryptography or, more specifically, private/public key cryptography that we send and receive bitcoin. You can liken a public key to your bank account number and a private key to your account password. By giving someone your public key, they can send you bitcoin. You can then use your private key to sign transactions (unlock your ability to spend) and spend your bitcoin.

Section Summary

Hopefully, by now, you've completed the border to the jigsaw puzzle that is Bitcoin. Over the following sections, we will fill in this puzzle so that by the end of the book, you will have a complete picture of how everything within the Bitcoin ecosystem intersects.

As highlighted at the start, our goal in this section is to introduce each of the key concepts that make up Bitcoin, so don't worry if things don't yet make sense. Bear with us as we explore these concepts in much more detail as we progress through the following chapters.

In the next chapter, we will step away from Bitcoin's history and start unravelling the intricacies of the protocol and technology underpinning this magic internet money.

CHAPTER 2

The Technology & Protocol Underpinning Bitcoin

"Any sufficiently advanced technology is indistinguishable from magic" - Arthur C. Clarke

SECTION 1

Decentralization

Key Questions Answered:
What is decentralization?
Why does Bitcoin need to be decentralized?
What makes Bitcoin decentralized?
How does Bitcoin solve the Byzantine Generals' Problem?

With chapter one behind us, it is time to explore the inner workings of Bitcoin.

We often hear of this concept of decentralization in relation to Bitcoin, with people placing a lot of emphasis on its importance. This section will examine what it is and why it is crucial, particularly for a monetary good.

Before diving in, we wanted to highlight that Bitcoin is incredibly interconnected. Understanding one part requires knowledge of another. It is, therefore, best to just jump straight in. With this in mind, you may have questions arise in the first few sections of this chapter, but we promise that with perseverance, those questions will be answered in the coming sections.

What is decentralization?

Before diving into decentralization as it relates to Bitcoin, let's go over what it is and how it differs from its counterpart, centralization. In its simplest form, decentralization can be described[15] as:

"The transfer of control and decision-making from a centralized entity (individual, organization, or group thereof) to a distributed network. Decentralized networks strive to reduce the level of trust that participants must place in one another."

In other words, decentralization involves distributing trust throughout the network rather than relying on any singular entity. The larger the distributed network, the more trustless it becomes.

This differs from a centralized system where trust is inherently required. A centralized entity places trust in a person or a small group of people to finalize any decisions impacting the network (which could be millions of people). We must have trust and faith that the central entity has our best interests at heart.

Centralization is excellent for entities that want to pivot quickly and test ideas, such as those in the tech world, where entrepreneurs create start-ups that test and produce wild, innovative ideas in short succession. However, rapid decision-making and quick pivoting are much harder under a decentralized system where change requires consensus amongst its participants. Since many people have different views, it can be challenging, or sometimes impossible, to shift gears quickly.

Decentralized systems foster a trustless environment where no single entity has control or can govern the direction of the network. This promotes security, stability and predictability. That's not to say a centralized system cannot have these things; it's just that a centralized entity differs in that it can shift gears, take its users by surprise, and make unilateral decisions that adversely affect users. This can have negative impacts on security, stability or predictability.

Let us now integrate Bitcoin into this topic of decentralization.

Why does Bitcoin need to be decentralized?

Every day we interact with centralized entities, such as our money, bank, cell phone provider, internet service provider etc. Our bank, for example, runs its own central ledger, which houses all of its customer's information and transaction history, including credit, debits, and current account balances.

One of the drawbacks to this is that an authoritative figure, such as the bank manager, has the ability to change the ledger. We, therefore, have to trust that there are no malicious individuals within the bank who would adjust the ledger to their benefit and at our expense. While one might argue that this is improbable, we simply want to highlight the fact that it is indeed possible.

With regard to money and monetary policy, we currently have little choice but to trust and rely on the government and the central bank. They control the monetary supply, interest rates, taxation, and government spending through monetary and fiscal policy. Tinkering with any of these levers can drastically impact the currency's purchasing power, diluting the value of the units of currency we hold.

As should now be evident, although there are benefits to centralization, most people desire security and stability when it comes to their savings. They want to trust that their purchasing power isn't going to decline through dilution one day or one year to the next and that their bank isn't going to close their bank account or reject their wire transfer. Because of this over-reliance on trust in our traditional system, Bitcoin was born. That said, in order to remove this reliance on trust, Bitcoin had to achieve decentralization.

You may wonder **if Satoshi created Bitcoin; doesn't that make it centralized?**

Although Satoshi wrote the initial software and rules of Bitcoin, he left the project within a couple of years. Since then, the 'community' (a worldwide, ad hoc group voluntarily engaging with the network) has been in charge of all decision-making and governance through consensus. We can only imagine that Satoshi knew that, in order for Bitcoin to grow into a truly decentralized network, he had to remove himself.

This is not the case for the vast majority of the other cryptocurrencies that exist today. Most of these can be characterized by having foundations or central bodies that govern the direction of the project, changing monetary policy as they see fit, reserving significant units of the currencies for founders or insiders, and can even change the history of transactions.

As a decentralized network, Bitcoin has proven itself when it comes to stability and security since its inception and has had virtually 100% uptime, except for a few brief moments in its very early days. Bitcoin has also never been hacked, which is a feat in itself, given that it is arguably the most scrutinized computer code in computer science history due to the value residing behind its transparent source code.

At this point, Satoshi could reveal himself tomorrow, but it wouldn't make a difference to the Bitcoin network. After he handed it over to the community, he conceded control. He, therefore, has no more authority over Bitcoin than you or I, or most importantly, any central banker.

What makes Bitcoin decentralized?

As we discussed in the previous section, two of the most essential elements in the Bitcoin network are:

1. **The Nodes** that enforce the rules of the network and monitor the blockchain, ensuring the transactions and miners are adhering to these rules.
2. **The Miners**, who confirm transactions by adding pending transactions to a new block and appending this new block to the blockchain, thus updating the ledger.

Combined, the nodes and miners create what is called a distributed ledger. And it is this distributed ledger that promotes a decentralized, or in other words, a trustless environment.

How does Bitcoin solve the Byzantine Generals' Problem?

If you recall from the previous section, "Bitcoin's Inception," we introduced the Byzantine General's Problem.

How can we send a message without the need for trust or a third party?

For Bitcoin to become truly decentralized, it had to solve this problem. Anyone must be able to send and receive bitcoin without the need for trust or a third party (like a bank).

And here's how it does so...

Within a centralized system, such as the bank, a central authority controls the ledger. We have to trust the bank's central authority. What Bitcoin does differently is:

1. It breaks up the centralized authority into two roles: **Rule enforcement**– the nodes, and **transaction confirmation and settlement**– the miners.
2. It then allows any number of everyday people to run a node or become a miner (or both).

We no longer have to rely on any single entity to ensure everyone follows the rules and that transactions are verified and settled honestly.

Let's expand on these two vital roles listed above:

Rule Enforcement (Nodes)

Every node in the Bitcoin network is a computer running freely available software, which features:

1. A copy of the Bitcoin rules, which the network has defined through consensus.
2. An up-to-date copy of the Bitcoin ledger, which details all transactions and balances (who owns what).

As mentioned before, no singular entity has control over the ledger. It is distributed amongst every single node in the network. Each node continuously checks its version of truth against everyone within the network. A bad actor could set up a node and change the rules, but if their rules don't align with the majority, their changes will be ignored by the Bitcoin network.

Transaction Confirmation & Settlement (Miners)

We will discuss mining in greater detail later. In the meantime, we are simplifying things here so that you understand the basic concept.

Each miner in the Bitcoin network is a special computer containing sophisticated hardware designed to solve an extremely complex computational problem.

Firstly, when Bitcoin miners create a new block, there is no certainty that they will be the ones to append this newly created block onto the blockchain. Why? Every miner has to compete against every other miner on the network by winning a cryptographic hashing lottery, where they need to guess a number below a certain target. The first miner to solve the problem is allowed to append their newly created block onto the blockchain, updating the ledger. As compensation, they collect the block reward, which includes all the transaction fees for every transaction within this new block and the block subsidy.

Secondly, every block and transaction is monitored by the nodes. A miner could, in theory, attempt to cheat the network by changing transaction details in their block to benefit themselves. For example, let's say there's a transaction where Sally sends Jill 0.001 bitcoin. The miner could alter the transaction to have Sally send the 0.001 bitcoin to themselves instead. However, as all transactions and blocks are monitored by the nodes (rule enforcers) and secured by cryptography, they would reject the miner's altered block. With this rejection, the miner would lose their compensation for creating a block. Therefore, it is in the miners' best interest to support the network rather than cheat it. Everyone is incentivized to play by the rules!

Combined, this updating of the ledger (transaction confirmation, settlement and rule enforcement) across a network that's spread across multiple locations and entities (miners and nodes) is known as distributed ledger technology. The more widely distributed the ledger is, the more stable, secure and decentralized Bitcoin becomes. This non-reliance on any singular or centralized entity is where the term "trustless" or "permissionless" comes from. You do not need to trust any central authority, and you do not require permission from any singular entity to transact on the network.

Distributed Ledger Example

This idea of distributed ledgers may seem a little abstract, so here's a scaled-down example of Bitcoin. Imagine we had our very own blockchain, just like Bitcoin. This blockchain contained some really important data we were working on. We could secure this data in a distributed way by keeping one copy at home and another on our office computer. We could then write a program (node) that would continuously compare these datasets and flag any discrepancies.

This is where the beauty of the distributed blockchain comes into play. We can compare these copies at any time by having multiple copies of the blockchain.

For example, let's imagine we leave our office computer unlocked, and some nefarious actor changes the data in our blockchain. Luckily, when we check our node, we will see that it has flagged a discrepancy between the office and home computers. However, now, we face the issue of which dataset is correct. The office or the home computer?

With only two versions of the data, we can't tell which copy of our blockchain the attacker has changed unless we personally know. But relying on our own knowledge means we are relying on trust. And, remember, we want this to be a trustless environment.

It would stand to reason that it would be handy if we had a third version to compare to. Therefore, let's keep a copy at home, a copy at the office and another copy at our friend's house.

If the nefarious actor were to strike again, we would now have a consensus mechanism by which to compare versions. If one computer is tampered with, the other two will show consensus on the datasets they are running, so we will know they are correct. We can, therefore, disregard the misaligned computer and continue on our way.

In this scenario, we still have to put a level of trust into this consensus by assuming that the nefarious actor would not have been able to:

1. Know the physical location of all three nodes in our network.
2. Be able to break in and change the data on two of the three sets of this blockchain.

Now imagine thousands of miners and nodes randomly distributed throughout the world, updating and verifying this blockchain. A bad actor would have to track down and change more than 50% of these nodes to cast doubt about which version of the chain was the truth. This is highly improbable, if not impossible, and is precisely how the Bitcoin blockchain works. A network of randomly distributed miners and nodes, run by everyday people, each storing a version of the truth and keeping each other honest. This is what makes bitcoin decentralized and trustless. No one party controls it, and it is distributed between each and every participant in the network.

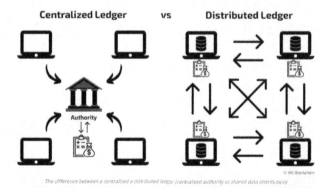

The difference between a centralised a distributed ledger (centralised authority vs shared data distribution)

Figure 2.11: *Centralized vs Decentralized* Ledgers[16]

Tying everything together, Bitcoin solves the Byzantine Generals' Problem of how to send a message/bitcoin without the need for trust or a third party, as we are never relying on any singular central authority to transact. When you send or receive bitcoin, your transaction is processed by a random miner on the network and then confirmed by every node (As of May 2022, there are over 15,000[17] reachable nodes and many more unreachable[18] nodes). With Bitcoin, there is no need for trust. In the words of Satoshi, Bitcoin is:

"a distributed system with no single point of failure. Users hold the crypto keys to their own money and transact directly with each other."

Bitcoin is the most decentralized and trustless monetary asset to have ever existed. This property, whereby Bitcoin' cannot be manipulated, co-opted or coerced by any single person, government, institution or entity, is what entices so many to join the network.

SECTION 2

Blockchain, Hashing & Mining

Key Questions Answered:
Why do we need miners?
What is the role of miners?
What is Hashing?
How is a blockchain secured?
How do blockchains prevent changes in previous information?

Chapter two brings us deeper into the nuts and bolts of how Bitcoin works from a protocol perspective. Let's jump into the blockchain, hashing and mining.

> **Side note:** Grey text is for a slightly more in-depth explanation.

Why do we need miners?

Miners are an integral component of the Bitcoin network. We need them to mine blocks, which leads to bitcoin issuance, and to confirm the transactions. Moreover, miners (along with nodes) help keep the network decentralized, as we do not have to trust any single authority. Instead, we can distribute this trust across a large, geographically dispersed network of miners, all incentivized to work toward a common goal.

What is the role of miners?

Before a bitcoin transaction can be completed, it must be added to the blockchain. Therefore, there are two states to bitcoin transactions:

1. **Unconfirmed** - After a transaction has been initiated, it "floats" in something called the memory pool, or "mempool," for short. There is no certainty that the transaction will be processed in this state. This is similar to a pending transaction on your credit card statement. Something could cause the transaction to be rejected or declined.

2. **Confirmed** - Once a transaction has been appended to the blockchain and checked by the nodes, the transaction is classified as "confirmed." While similar to a posted transaction on your credit card statement, it differs in that it is almost impossible to reverse a bitcoin transaction.

Roughly every ten minutes, a new block is added to the blockchain. It is the role of the miners to take unconfirmed transactions from the mempool, add them to a block and then compete against one another to have their block appended to the blockchain. The miner who wins is awarded the block reward (currently 6.25 bitcoin plus the transaction fees).

Now that we understand why we need miners and their role in the network, you're probably wondering how they actually conduct this work we know as "mining?"

Let's explore what mining entails.

What is Hashing?

Before we can begin to unpack mining, we must first grasp a critical concept used in Bitcoin called "hashing." Hashing is the act of sending information through a hash function. Think of hashing as creating a unique digital fingerprint from a data set.

A hash function works as follows:
1.   Input data goes into the hash function.
2.   Within this hash function, the input data is sent through a bunch of mathematical processes.
3.   The output is a series of alphanumeric characters known as the hash.

If we were to input "Looking Glass education is the best!" into a SHA256 hash function (which is the hash function currently used in Bitcoin), we would be returned with the following:

"818a628787a0c0933c84cca11aa7e846d35928cd0ef7e8162961a1e-7ab119772"

This string of letters and numbers is called the "hash."

Despite the hash looking like a mixture of letters and numbers, it is essential to note that it is simply a number represented in hexadecimal form (we explain this soon), and therefore, it has a value. This will be crucial to remember for later.

Let's recap:

- **Hash Function** - A series of mathematical processes which convert input data into a hash (A digital fingerprint of the information).
- **Hashing** - The act of sending data through a hash function and generating a hash.
- **Input Data** - The information being sent into the hash function.
- **Hash** - The output of the hash function.

Why do we use hash functions?

Security

Hashing allows us to verify sensitive information without revealing/ disclosing the information itself. For example, a website may not want to store your password for privacy reasons. It, therefore, keeps a hash of your password on file. Every time you log into the website, you enter your password, which is sent through the same hash function that was used when you first set your password. If the hash generated matches the hash on file, you are granted access. If not, it knows that you entered the wrong password and denies you entry.

It is important to highlight that a hash is a one-way function. In other words, knowing the hash doesn't allow us to determine the input data, i.e. in the above example, there is no way of decrypting the password from knowing the hash. This is the power of cryptography.

Efficiency

Hashing allows us to generate a digital fingerprint from any volume of input data, saving time and energy when comparing data. For example, if we had two large bodies of information and we wanted to confirm that the information contained in each set was identical, we could send each set through a hash function and instantly see if the hashes returned were the same. This is far more efficient than comparing and analyzing the input data manually.

The SHA256 Hash Function

There are many different types of hash functions, all serving different purposes, and some are better than others. The Bitcoin protocol uses one called SHA256, which was invented in 2001 by the US Government's National Security Agency (NSA). It is well known to be incredibly safe, secure and resilient.

What is fascinating about hashing is that it doesn't matter how much data you run through the hash function. The output is always the same length (see figure 2.21). Even though "Example 1" has more input data than "Example 2," the hash length remains the same at 64 characters.

*Give it a try yourself! Here[19] is a link to an online SHA256 Hash Function. Play around with entering various information and notice how the hash changes, even when you simply capitalize a letter.

Why is a hash output always the same length? First, a SHA256 hash will only ever include the characters 0123456789ABCDEF. This character format is called base 16 or hexadecimal, as there are 16 characters. Secondly, the "256" in SHA256 refers to the size of the hash. No matter how much data goes into the hash function, the output will always be 256 bits in size.

What does that mean? Bits are binary units. They can either be a 0 or a 1. The hash function in binary would be 256 characters long, consisting of 0's and 1's. A 256-bit long number can be better represented using a hexadecimal number consisting of just 64 characters. Although interesting, all you really need to know is that a SHA256 hash will always be 64 hexadecimal characters in length, no matter how much input data goes into the hash function.

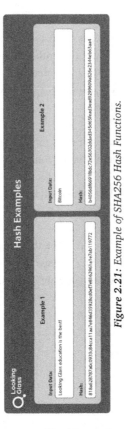

Figure 2.21: Example of SHA256 Hash Functions.

Now that we have a firm grasp of hashing and some of the key features of the SHA256 hash function, let's dive into blocks and mining.

About Blocks

As you can probably guess, Bitcoin's blockchain is made up of many, many blocks (745,555 at the time of writing, July 2022). Within each of these blocks is a myriad of important information, including a list of transactions. That means that if we were to look inside every one of the 745,555 blocks, we could piece together every bitcoin transaction that has ever taken place.

It is the role of the miners to create these blocks and append their newly created blocks to the blockchain. Whenever a new block is added to the blockchain, all of the previously unconfirmed transactions that the miner has recorded in this new block become confirmed. This process is known as settlement. Once a transaction is added to a block and appended to the blockchain, it is recorded on the Bitcoin blockchain forever. This transaction is now final and is almost impossible to reverse. This may seem a little abstract, so let's look at an example.

Figure 2.22 is an example of a simplified block. For simplicity, let's ignore all of the information under the "Block Header" and just focus on the "Transaction Data" and "Block Hash."

If we ignore the "Block Header" information, for now, notice how we have something very similar to figure 2.21. We have input data, labelled "Transaction Data" (1.), and we have an output hash, labelled "Block Hash" (2.) If you recall, a hash is simply a digital fingerprint of the input data and "Block Hash" (2.) is the digital fingerprint of our "Transaction Data" (1.). Comparing "Example 1" and "Example 2" above, you will notice each "Block Hash" output is unique, as the input "Transaction Data" within each block is different.

Without going into the details of the "Block Header" just yet, it is important to note that the "Block Hash" is a digital fingerprint of the entire block. That means it includes all of the "Transaction Data" and "Block Header" information. If any single piece of this information in the "Block Header" or "Transaction Data" changes, the "Block Hash" will reflect this and change.

You're probably wondering, well, this is just one block. What makes a blockchain?

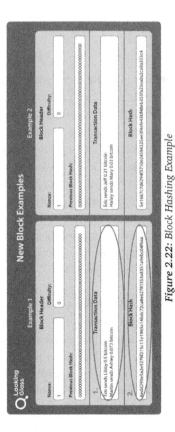

Figure 2.22: Block Hashing Example

Blockchain

Let's picture a metal chain (Figure 2.23). With this image in your mind, notice how it is made up of many links chained together.

This is a good metaphor for the blockchain. Think of each block as an integral link within the blockchain as a whole. The only difference is that, instead of the blocks being connected via a physical metallic loop, they're connected by an information field known as the "Previous Block Hash" (1.), which references the prior block's "Block Hash," as shown below.

Figure 2.23: *A Physical Metal Chain*

Figure 2.24 is an example of a three-block-long blockchain where "Block 3" references "Block 2," which references "Block 1".

The output "Block Hash" from "Block 1" now forms part of the input data for "Block 2's" "Block Hash." Once "Block 2" has been appended to the blockchain, its "Block Hash" forms the input data for "Block 3" and on we go, forming a chain.

Altered Block

Where a distributed blockchain ledger differs from a simple, centralized ledger is that once a block is appended to the distributed blockchain, it becomes almost impossible to alter any information stored in these blocks. This is not the case for a centralized ledger, where it is easy to go back and modify the ledger, as this information is not distributed or repeatedly referenced and checked for accuracy by thousands of geographically dispersed parties.

In figure 2.25, if we were to accidentally reorder the transactions in "Block 1" so that Martin's transaction was first (1.), instead of Tim's (such as in the "Blockchain Example" above), the "Block Hash" would change (3.).

We now face a problem. The "Previous Block Hash" field in "Block 2" (2.) no longer accurately references the "Block Hash" of "Block 1" (3.). The blockchain has been broken. To fix this, we would have to alter every proceeding block until they are correctly linked once again—a tiresome task (we will explore why in a moment).

Now that we are clear about how blocks make up the blockchain, let's look at mining and how these miners, all with a copy of the blockchain, compete against one another to append to the Bitcoin blockchain.

Mining

When miners create a new block, there is no certainty that they will be the ones to append this newly created block onto the blockchain. Why is this? Every miner has to compete against every other miner on the network by solving a computational problem.

The first miner to do so appends their newly created block onto the blockchain and then broadcasts this update to everyone else on the network. Once the network confirms that this new block is indeed legitimate, the successful miner collects the block reward (made up of the block subsidy, currently 6.25 bitcoin, and the transaction fees) as compensation for their work.

If you recall, earlier, we mentioned that the "Block Hash" is simply a number. Understanding this is essential as it helps us grasp this concept of the mining competition.

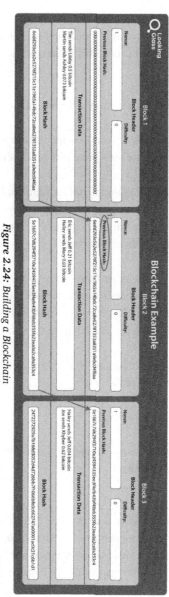

Figure 2.24: Building a Blockchain

So, what is this competition? In its simplest form, miners have to get their "Block Hash" below a target value, and the "Difficulty" determines this value. We don't expect this to make sense initially, so let's use an analogy.

You could liken mining to a unique golf tournament:

Imagine a bunch of golfers (miners) competing against one another to win (mine a block) and receive a prize (the block reward).

The only difference to a traditional golf tournament is that, rather than the winner being the lowest-scoring player over 18 holes by the end of the tournament, the winner is the first to score under a target amount of points (the "Difficulty Target").

Additionally, this point target isn't fixed. The more players in the tournament, the higher the probability someone will score under the point target. Therefore, as more players compete (more miners), the target number decreases, making the game harder to win.

Lastly, if you don't score under the point target, you can play again, and as many times as you like.

This is essentially Bitcoin mining.

Confused? We get it. These can be very abstract concepts to grasp, so let's break them down further.

Difficulty Target

So what does it mean for miners to get their "Block Hash" below a target value? You may have noticed that a hash is hexadecimal, meaning it contains both numbers and letters. However, although the hash contains letters, it is still a numerical value. To help visualize this, figure 2.26 is a chart showing the base 16 hexadecimal characters converted

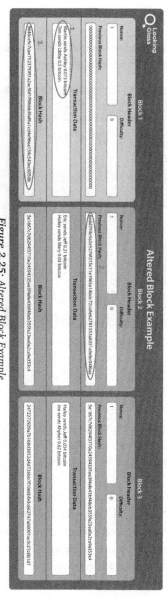

Figure 2.25: *Altered Block Example*

to their numerical value.

Don't worry. You don't need to remember this conversion. It just helps when understanding the difficulty adjustment.

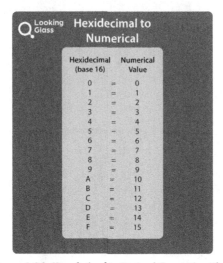

Figure 2.26: Hexadecimal to Decimal Conversion Chart

Knowing that the "Block Hash" is simply a value allows us to better understand the role "Difficulty" plays.

As described in the golfing example above, for a miner to win the competition and append their block onto the blockchain, they have to generate a "Block Hash" value below the current target value.

This is achieved through a numerical text string of data within the block known as the "nonce". If you recall, the "Block Hash" is a digital fingerprint of all the information contained in a block. However, although there are multiple pieces of information contained in a block, only one of them can be manually altered, the "Nonce." Changing the "Nonce" value from, say, 0 to 1 is going to change the entire "Block

Hash".

This is where the game of trial and error comes in. As there's no way to predict the output of a hash function, miners must continue entering arbitrary numbers into the "Nonce" field until they manage to get their "Block Hash" value below the target number. The "Difficulty" sets the target value for the block.

Mining is essentially the biggest guessing game on the planet.

Let's have a look at the example in figure 2.27. For simplicity, instead of using the standard 64-character SHA256 hash, let's pretend the "Block Hash" is a value between 0 and 9999. In this instance, the "Difficulty" is set at 0085 (1.). This means the first miner to get their "Block Hash" value below the target value of 0085 gets to append their block onto the blockchain. Therefore, the miner will continue to adjust their "Nonce" value until they generate a "Block Hash" that is below 0085 or 85.

As you can see, initially (2.), the miner is unsuccessful. A "Nonce" value of one gives the miner a "Block Hash" value of 6345. This is not below the desired value of 0085. The miner keeps incrementing the nonce by one each time. 2,3,4,5,6…etc. is attempted. After 356 attempts (3.), the miner has managed to find a "Nonce" value that gives the "Block Hash" a value of 0049, below the target value. And lucky for them, they are the first miner to do so. Therefore, they append their block to the blockchain, broadcast the new block to everyone else on the network, and are compensated with the block reward.

At this point, every other miner on the network discards their current block and starts working on a new block, referencing this newly appended block, and the competition starts again.

The network is then able to verify that this new block is valid by confirming the block data coupled with the nonce produces a valid hash lower than the target. One of the magical features of cryptography is that the network is able to confirm the nonce is valid without having to repeat the work that was done to discover it.

We liken this to those wiz-kids who can solve a Rubik's cube. We have no idea what steps they took to solve the jumbled puzzle, but we can easily confirm they solved it by looking at it.

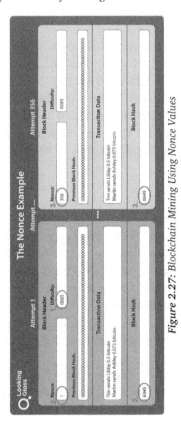

Figure 2.27: Blockchain Mining Using Nonce Values

In figure 2.27, you may have noticed above that as the "Difficulty" increases, the target value decreases, thereby requiring more leading zeros at the start of the "Block Hash" (3.). With this in mind, we can gauge the current difficulty for miners. At the time of writing, the target number is 45 characters long. Given that a SHA256 hash is 64 characters long, the "Block Hash" has to start with at least 19 leading zeros (64 - 45 = 19) for its value to be below the target number. As SHA256 uses base 16, each character has the potential to be one of 16 different characters, zero being one of those characters. From a probabilistic standpoint, the chance of a hash starting with one leading zero is 1/16 (6.25%), two leading zeros is 1/256 (0.39%), and three leading zeros is 1/4,096 (0.02%). 19 leading zeros is an improbable 1/75,557,863,725,914,300,000,000. As more leading zeroes are required, it is exponentially harder to get the "Block Hash" below the target number.

How does the "Difficulty" value change?

Every 2016 blocks (roughly two weeks), the Bitcoin code undergoes a "Difficulty Adjustment" to ensure that blocks are mined at an average of ten minutes per block.

If many miners suddenly came online, more competition would mean blocks would be mined faster than every ten minutes. To prevent this, at the next "Difficulty Adjustment," the difficulty would increase (lower target value) to counteract this rise in block production. This makes it harder for miners to generate a hash that satisfies this lower target value, thus slowing down the mining.

Alternatively, if many miners were to go offline (as we saw in the great Chinese mining ban of 2021) due to the sudden reduction in competition, blocks would be mined slower than every ten minutes, as the difficulty would be too hard for those remaining on the network. In this scenario, the next difficulty adjustment would decrease the difficulty, thus increasing the target number and making it easier for miners to mine once again.

Bad Actor

Building on our altered block example earlier, as every block references the "Block Hash" of the previous block, if a nefarious actor were to change any single piece of data in any block on the blockchain, it would immediately break every block thereafter. This is because if you change a piece of information in a block, the "Block Hash" will reflect this, and the "Previous Block Hash" field in the following block will no longer match the "Block Hash" of the changed block.

We can see this in figure 2.28, where the "Block Hash" of "Block 1" (3.) does not match the "Previous Block Hash" of "Block 2" (2.). The blockchain has been broken.

What is happening here? In our "Blockchain Example" earlier, under "Block 1," Martin had sent Ashley 0.073 bitcoin. However, what if Ashley was a miner and decided to adjust the transaction? Let's have a look.

In figure 2.28, suppose Ashley changed the transaction so that Martin, without his consent, sent her 1.073 bitcoin instead. The "Block Hash" of "Block 1" (1.) would change to reflect this. However, in doing so, the "Previous Block Hash" in "Block 2" (2.) would no longer match the "Block Hash" of "Block 1" (3.). The blockchain has been broken. Nothing is connecting "Block 2" to "Block 1." For Ashley to keep the blockchain intact, she would have to update every block following the changed block. That would be a significant task! Let's have a look at why this is an uphill battle.

Nodes

If you recall from our example of the distributed ledger in "Decentralization," every node carries a copy of the ledger. If a miner were to alter a block, it would immediately be flagged and discarded by the nodes, as that miner's copy of the ledger would be out of consensus with the rest of the network.

Longest Chain

Miners communicate with the Bitcoin network when they append a new block onto the blockchain, letting everybody know that they successfully generated a "Block Hash" below the target value. This communication consists of broadcasting their new block to the network.

At this point, the nodes update their ledgers, and every miner stops working on their current block, looks toward the longest, verified version of the blockchain and starts working on a new block.

It's important to highlight that miners will always work on the longest chain, known as the main chain. If they're not working on the main chain, the nodes will reject any changes they make, and their endeavours will be fruitless.

With this new understanding, if a nefarious miner decides to go back and alter an older block, not only would they have to first change the contents of the block to get the "Block Hash" below the target number, but they would have to do this for every successive block, expending an immense amount of energy.

Another way to look at this is that in order for their altered blockchain to compete with the main chain (longest chain), they'd have to mine the altered block and subsequent blocks faster than the entire network is mining blocks until their chain became longer than the main chain. This means that one bad actor would have to expend more than the equivalent energy that it took the entire network of miners to build the blockchain from the point of change.

A tall order, if not virtually impossible! Wouldn't they be better off simply pointing their hash power toward solving new blocks and dominating the competition for block rewards?

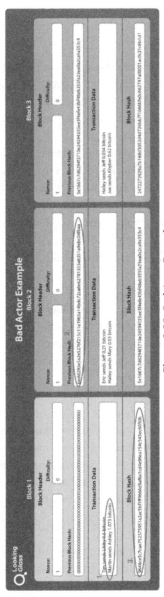

Figure 2.28: Bad Actor Example

Fun Fact: A little-known fact is that this process of committing transactions to the blockchain, requiring all transactions to be audited every ten minutes, birthed the concept of "triple entry accounting[20]." This is the first major innovation in the structure of accounting since double-entry bookkeeping, which was introduced in 1494.

Section Summary

With the protocol randomizing which miner verifies each block, miners are incentivized to act honestly and in the interest of the community. If they fail to do so, their newly mined block will be reversed, and they will lose the block reward.

As a result of this randomization, we do not have to rely on any single miner to process our transactions. It is for this reason we can say, "Bitcoin allows us to transact in a trustless and permissionless manner."

Without this randomized transaction settlement, we must lean on trusted third parties to process our transactions, and then the question is, "can they be trusted to act in the interest of the user?"

Side Note: The bad actor example given above is not entirely accurate. Miners are limited in what information they can alter. Transactions are something they cannot alter. We'll go into this in more detail soon. For now, just know that only the bitcoin owner can sign/send their bitcoin. If the miner alters the transaction, it invalidates the transaction as the altered transaction has not been "signed" by the owner of that bitcoin.

SECTION 3

The Supply

Key Questions Answered:
How does new bitcoin come into existence?
Why will there only ever be 21 million bitcoin?
Do halvings impact the price?
How does the difficulty adjustment regulate the amount of
bitcoin mined?

In the previous section, we dove deep into the functionality of Bitcoin miners and how they keep the Bitcoin network secure. Hopefully, you now have much greater clarity as to the inner workings of the block-chain. Let us now dive into the bitcoin supply and the release of virgin bitcoin.

How does new bitcoin come into existence?

If you recall, when a miner wins in this competition of hashing computation, they get to append the block they've been working on onto the blockchain. At this point, all the transactions inside of that block move from unconfirmed in the memory pool to confirmed and verified on the blockchain.

What is in it for the miners? As discussed, the miner is rewarded with what is known as the "block reward." This reward contains all of the transaction fees associated with every transaction in the block, and, more importantly, it contains the block subsidy. It is through the block subsidy that new bitcoin enters into circulation.

Let's explore this.

Coinbase Transaction
The first transaction inside every block is known as the coinbase transaction. This differs from a regular transaction, which requires two parties, the sender and the receiver. For the coinbase transaction, there is only one party, the miner, who was successful in mining the block.

A coinbase transaction, also known as a generating transaction, is fundamental in the generation of new bitcoin. In other words, it is the coinbase transaction that is responsible for the birthing of virgin coins.

We can see the coinbase transaction for block 736,837 (just an arbitrary block we chose to examine) in figure 2.31. We are using the data obtained from a blockchain explorer, which is a 3rd party service that helps us explore the blockchain data with a nice user interface.

When we compare the two transactions below, notice the differences. The second transaction has a red arrow for the sending party and two green arrows for the receiving parties. However, in the first transaction, there is only a green arrow, the miner's wallet and a grey arrow that says "Coinbase (Newly Generated Coins)."

These newly generated coins have been introduced through the Bitcoin Protocol as part of the predetermined release schedule of bitcoin.

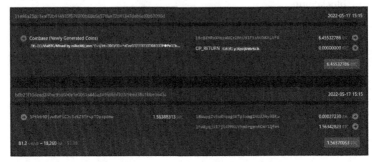

Figure 2.31: Bitcoin Block

What is important to note is that not all of the 6.45532786 bitcoin shown above are newly created bitcoin.

If you recall, the block reward contains both the block subsidy + the transaction fees. Therefore, out of the 6.45532786 bitcoin the miner received, 6.25 are the block subsidy (virgin bitcoin), and 0.2032786 are the combined total of the transaction fees for every transaction included in the block. You may now be wondering, how did the first bitcoin come into existence?

Genesis Block

The genesis block is a unique block in the Bitcoin blockchain as it is the first-ever block. However, although the genesis block is the first block, it is numbered block 0. If you recall, blocks store transactions and are linked to one another via the "Previous Block Hash" field. The only exception to this rule is for the genesis block, as it had no other block to link to and no transactions to record. Additionally, the first block was not actually mined. Instead, Satoshi hardcoded the block into the original Bitcoin software. He then used block 0 as the reference for the next block. It is from this point on that Bitcoin mining began.

It is easy to dismiss the first block as being just that, the first block. However, there is a lot of mystery and intrigue surrounding the genesis block. Pushing aside the fact that it is the first-ever block, the block has some quirks. For instance, before the genesis block, there was no such thing as Bitcoin and no bitcoin in existence. This changed with the genesis block, as it contained the first 50 bitcoin.

However, what's unique about the first block is that the bitcoin unearthed are unspendable. The coinbase transaction in block 0 for the first 50 bitcoin cannot be found in the ledger making the bitcoin unusable[21].

Whether Satoshi did this intentionally or not, we will never know. But it is often thought that Satoshi made this block reward unspendable so as not to obtain an unfair advantage in coin circulation. This practice is known as a pre-mine, which, although often frowned upon within the cryptocurrency space, is, unfortunately, a widespread practice. Anyone participating in the cryptocurrency space should make themself aware of this practice and how it may affect them.

Therefore, the first true spendable bitcoin were actually in block one (the second block).

Fun Fact: If you want to check out the genesis block, you can view the block here[22].

You're probably now thinking to yourself, "ok, ok, I understand how the first bitcoin were created, but if there can only ever be 21 million bitcoin, how can we continue to reward miners indefinitely?"

Why will there only ever be 21 million bitcoin?

Earlier, we highlighted that the current block subsidy is 6.25 bitcoin, but then we mentioned that the genesis block had a subsidy of 50 bitcoin. Well, which is it? What caps the total supply of bitcoin to 21 million is that the block subsidy diminishes over time, eventually trending to zero. At that point, we will have mined every bitcoin. This diminishing subsidy is a result of something known as the halvings.

Halvings

Every 210,000 blocks (roughly every four years), the block subsidy halves. This is known as a halving. These halvings will continue for a total of 32 halvings until around the year 2140. At this point, the block subsidy will no longer exist, and miners will only receive transaction fees in a block reward.

With no block subsidy, the total bitcoin in circulation will come to rest at just shy of 21 million, 20,999,999.9769[23], to be precise.

In figure 2.32, we can see the first 14 halving events. The orange line indicates the block subsidy, and the blue line shows the current supply of bitcoin. With a current block subsidy of 6.25 bitcoin, we can determine that we have experienced three halvings since Bitcoin's inception. The next halving will be at block 840,000 (~March 2024), where the block subsidy will decrease to 3.125 bitcoin.

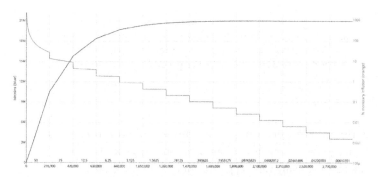

Figure 2.32: *Bitcoin Halving Events[24]*

Do halvings impact the price of bitcoin?

Every time there has been a halving so far, the price of bitcoin has sub-sequently run up. One reason for this is that each time we go through a halving event, the reward to miners (block subsidy) is halved. With miners only receiving half of what they were previously compensated, the cost to mine bitcoin increases. This increase in cost and reduced supply translates to higher prices. Why? If we assume that the costs to mine bitcoin remain fixed and the reward for their effort is halved, in theory, miners will demand at least double the price for their bitcoin to cover their overheads. In reality, while the actual price fluctuations vary, we can't ignore the impact that a reduced supply has on the sup-ply/demand economics with regard to bitcoin's price.

Fun Fact: People often say, "NgU (number go up)" or "bitcoin is mathematically programmed to go up in price." What they are referring to is the fact that because the block subsidy is programmatically halved every 210,000 blocks, we essentially have a pre-programmed supply constriction every four years, pushing up the price. Thinking about the supply and demand equilibrium dynamic that exists for goods and services, if demand remains constant and supply is reduced, this results in higher prices. Ask yourself, do you think the demand for bitcoin will go up or go down in the coming years?

Is the maximum supply of 21 million bitcoin really fixed?

Although Bitcoiners disagree at times, one belief has held true amongst the many varying personalities in the ecosystem. That is this belief in a fixed total supply, making bitcoin a truly scarce asset.

To be clear, it is not impossible for there to be more than 21 million bitcoin. Any changes to the Bitcoin protocol are voted on through consensus, so if we were to reach a majority consensus through all the nodes on the network, we could, in theory, raise the total supply of bitcoin.

However, this is highly, highly unlikely, as it is one of the most valued characteristics of Bitcoin. In fact, many Bitcoiners believe the issues we currently face in our global economy are directly related to our inflationary fiat currencies*.

*For more information on the effects of inflationary currencies, check out our "Debt, Inflation and the Bigger Picture[25]" course.

How does the difficulty adjustment regulate the amount of bitcoin mined?

In the previous section, we only briefly touched on the difficulty adjustment as we wanted to focus on the act of mining. However, it is imperative that we circle back as without this part of the protocol known as the difficulty adjustment, there is nothing stopping miners from continually mining blocks at an increasing rate, speeding up the issuance of bitcoin.

Every second of every day, miners globally compete to append their block to the blockchain. They expend energy hashing in an attempt to get their "Block Hash" below the target value. Collectively the total hashing by the network of miners is known as the "hash rate."

The hash rate can increase in two ways:
1.   More miners come on board, dedicating more energy and computational power to the network.
2.   The efficiency of the chips in these mining machines increases, allowing miners to raise their hash rate with the same or lower energy usage.

However, if there were no mechanism to increase the mining difficulty as more miners competed, we would face a problem. As the hash rate increased, blocks would be mined at an ever-increasing rate. As more bitcoin are mined, the price of bitcoin would collapse as miners flood the market to sell their bitcoin. What prevents this is a mechanism known as the difficulty adjustment, which regulates the block time, and, thereby, the issuance of new bitcoin.

Difficulty Adjustment
Every 2,016 blocks, roughly two weeks, the Bitcoin code calculates the average block time for the preceding 2,016 blocks. If, on average, blocks are being mined faster than every ten minutes, the difficulty increases, making it harder for miners to get their "Block Hash" below the target number. On the flip side, if the average block time exceeds ten minutes, the difficulty eases off, making it easier for miners. Although there is usually some variance in the block time, the difficulty adjustment makes for a predictable, almost systematic ten-minute block interval over the long run.

Fun fact: As outlined above, for every 2016 blocks, the Bitcoin mining difficulty is adjusted to maintain block time and supply issuance. In 1933, The US government Executive Order 6102 forbade the personal holding of gold by citizens. Many Bitcoiners speculate that this value of 2016 was not chosen randomly, but rather it is the reverse of 6102, and is a cheeky reference to one of the great innovations of Bitcoin, the ability to "self-custody" (explained in depth a little later on).

Ignoring all the confusing numbers in figure 2.33, we can see that the difficulty mimics the hash rate. As the hash rate fluctuates, the network difficulty reflects this. This ensures that blocks are being produced every ten minutes.

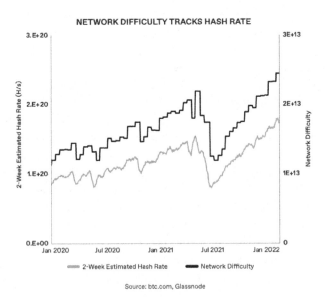

Figure 2.33: Network Difficulty[26]

This difficulty adjustment is unlike anything we have ever seen before.

Take gold, for example. If the price of gold were to increase, mining would become more favourable. As more gold miners search for this lucrative precious metal, more gold will be mined, increasing the total supply. This is not possible for Bitcoin. If the price of bitcoin went up 1000% tomorrow, miners would naturally flood into mining Bitcoin. However, no matter how much the hash rate increased, the difficulty to mine gets adjusted every two weeks, ensuring a predictable supply of bitcoin over time.

Section Summary

As you can see, the halvings and difficulty adjustment are vital for Bitcoin's supply schedule. Combined, they create a consistent and predictable release of bitcoin into the world.

The difficulty adjustment ensures an average block time of ten minutes, while the halving slowly reduces the block subsidy until the total supply of bitcoin eventually stops just shy of 21 million.

This scarcity is unique, and not only to the digital realm. When it comes to gold, we cannot be certain we will not find large reserves on this or other planets, thereby defeating its value proposition. But even then, without brand new large deposits, the gold supply has been growing at 1-2% per year since the early 1900s.

With the combination of an immutable ledger, a fixed cap supply of 21 million and the difficulty adjustment, we know exactly how much bitcoin there currently are, and we can predict the supply rate into the future with near pinpoint accuracy. Something that has previously not been possible.

SECTION 4

Public/Private Key Cryptography

Key Questions Answered:
What on earth even is a bitcoin?
What is a Private/Public Key Pair
What are bitcoin addresses?

So far, we have looked at the functionality of the blockchain and introduced the concept of distributed ledger technology. As a result, we should now have an understanding that within the Bitcoin Ledger exists a record of who owns what and that each new block updates the current state of ownership, that is, the transactions that occurred since the last block. Let's now focus on ownership and the sending and receiving of bitcoin.

Once again, we try not to get too technical and attempt to remove as much jargon as possible. At the same time, the truth is that this is a deep and complex topic. We will, therefore, do our best to provide the information needed for a deeper understanding of what Bitcoin is and how it works without trying to give you a dual degree in computer science and cryptography!

What on earth even is a bitcoin?

One of the biggest misconceptions surrounding Bitcoin is that people liken it to some type of file, such as a JPEG or an MP3, believing that when we send bitcoin, we're simply sending this JPEG or MP3 to someone else. You are also not alone if you view it as a digital coin you store on your computer, since this is how bitcoin is often portrayed in mainstream media. With this in mind, let's explore what bitcoin really is and how we transact using it!

Figure 2.41: Bitcoin

Latest transactions			
TXID	**Amount**	**USD**	**Fee**
e14d6...142b8	0.0209 BTC	$406	13.1 sat/vB
34c70...6b35c	1.1793 BTC	$22,853	5.03 sat/vB
ab160...28840	0.0038 BTC	$75	9.96 sat/vB
a8336...d80e6	0.081 BTC	$1,570	13.0 sat/vB
8df4a...ede9b	2.0028 BTC	$38,811	5.08 sat/vB
4ee2b...b2558	0.0059 BTC	$115	7.97 sat/vB

Figure 2.42: The Latest Bitcoin Transactions

When we log into our digital banking platform, we see all our accounts and the money in each one. It can be hard to believe, but this money is not linked to physical currency stored in a vault for safekeeping. Instead, the bank operates a central ledger which tracks how much money the bank owes to each account. When you send money to another person, nothing physically changes hands. Instead, money is debited from your account and credited to your friend's account. This transaction is then added to the bank's ledger, updating our balances.

> **Fun fact:** When you deposit money in a bank account, the money becomes the property of the bank. The account balances shown to you are simply an 'IOU' or a promise to pay you back (providing they have the funds or nothing else prevents this, such as government intervention!).

One of the roles of the bank is to ensure that only you, the account owner, have access to and can spend your funds. That means that if the bank suspects a transaction to be fraudulent or that we are not the true owner of the account from which we are trying to send money, they can freeze or even reverse the transaction.

In terms of the ledger, Bitcoin works in a similar way. When we send bitcoin to a friend, a new transaction is generated, updating the Bitcoin ledger. This transaction debits bitcoin from our account and credits bitcoin to our friend's account. Nothing tangible is exchanged. Instead, this new transaction has updated each of our balances. Bitcoin is simply a distributed ledger of records that keeps track of who owns what. Where Bitcoin differs is that there is no reliance on banks or trusted third parties.

This brings up the question: if we remove the banks and other third parties, how do we ensure that people can only spend their own bitcoin? This is where the power of cryptography comes in.

Bitcoin Addresses

Public Key

We will simplify the receiving of bitcoin down to the public key. However, as we will explore in time, this isn't necessarily accurate as to receive bitcoin, we must provide something known as a public address– a hash of our public key. So don't get too bogged down by public keys.

If we want to send money to a friend through our traditional banking system, we need to know their bank account number. Think of their bank account number as an address we can use to send the money. Bitcoin is no different. When we send bitcoin to a friend, we need to know their bitcoin address. This address is known as their public key.

Just like a bank account number, knowing someone's Bitcoin public key doesn't allow us to do anything with the funds inside this address/account. The only thing we can do is send bitcoin to this address.

Where a Bitcoin address differs from a bank account number is that knowing someone's address allows us to look it up on the Bitcoin Blockchain and see how much is stored at this address. However, since no names are reflected on the blockchain, it is impossible to determine who owns that address unless the account owner lets us know they are the owner. This makes the Bitcoin ledger pseudonymous rather than anonymous. For this reason, performing an illicit activity using Bitcoin is not a good idea, as every transaction is recorded forever. If the identity of the account owner becomes known at any point in the future, all their transactions will be visible for the world to see. There are ways to improve privacy once you understand what you are doing, but that is outside the scope of this book.

Private Keys

You're probably thinking, "Ok, I understand if I give someone my public key, I can receive bitcoin, but how do I send someone bitcoin?"

This is where the private key comes in. You can liken a Bitcoin private key to an internet banking password. If our friend gives us their bank account number, we can't do much except send them money. However, if they give us their bank account number and internet banking password, we can go into their account and start spending their money. Just like you wouldn't give anyone the password to your internet banking, you should NEVER give someone your private key.

To drive home the message, if someone manages to obtain your internet banking password and therefore account access, as mentioned above, the bank could freeze or reverse the transaction if they believed the transaction to be fraudulent. This is because your bank account is connected to you as an individual and the bank has some degree of responsibility to ensure fraud is minimized. When you signed up for the account, you had to provide your identification and sign several documents.

This is not the case for bitcoin. Anyone can create a bitcoin address at any time and have money sent to that address. The only thing that makes you the owner of that address is that you hold the private key, which gives you the right to spend the corresponding bitcoin. However, if someone else gets hold of this private key, they too can spend that bitcoin, and, unlike our traditional banking system, there is no way to freeze or reverse a transaction. To reiterate, NEVER share your Private Key with anyone.

So... what exactly is a private key?

Simply put, it is your password to your funds in the form of a massive unique number, a number so large that even if <u>every computer on earth</u>[27] tried to guess your password, it would still take an unfathomable amount of time. The number is so large that it is comparable to the number of atoms in the universe. Guessing a private key is akin to finding that one atom in the universe or winning Powerball 9 times in a row! While we can't say it's impossible, it is highly, highly improbable.

And, just like no two atoms are the same, no two private keys are the same. Each is completely unique.

A private key is a 256-bit binary number. In other words, it is a string of 256 ones and zeros. This can be represented in binary format, decimal or, more commonly, hexadecimally. Although we have previously introduced these concepts while exploring mining, here are some more examples.

Below is the same randomly generated private key in Binary, Decimal and Hexadecimal format. (No, there is no bitcoin assigned to this key, trust us, we looked)

Binary:
11011010010001101011010101011001111100100001101100111110100010101010110111011000110010010010111001001011001001010110001011100001110110011110101011100101111111000011011111100110111010001101101010100001000001001011000011100111001110010110000000010011110110110010

Decimal:
98729131926707364344155946614204368554393612909660450514900410658357640330085

Hexadecimal:
DA46B559F21B3E955BB1925C964AC5C3B3D72FE1BF37476A104B0-

E7396027B65

If this is confusing, you could liken each representation of our private key to a different language. You could say, "hello, hola, bonjour or asalaam alaikum." While some are longer than others, they all mean the same thing. With this in mind, you might notice that it is more convenient to represent a private key in hexadecimal format, as it uses fewer characters to represent the same data.

What's more, as a copy of the blockchain is data stored on every node that chooses to run it, the developers always look for the most efficient way of representing this data to minimize data storage requirements. "Wait, so are you telling me that the hexadecimal number above is my password? How can I remember that?" We agree that even in its simplest hexadecimal form, it is doubtful you'll be able to remember your private key. With this in mind, you can convert any private key into what is known as a seed phrase. Again, this is just another representation of the same private key.

Seed Phrase:
vessel catch dilemma club armor alley lumber donor twin divide account globe

These words are known as BIP39[28]. What's interesting to point out is that these words are not random. When converting your private key into a seed phrase, there are a total of 2048 potential words that can make up your seed phrase (private key), with the first four letters of each word being unique. Therefore, if you wanted to, you could simply write down or remember the first four letters of each word, although this is not generally recommended.

Fun Exercise: Get a coin, a pen and a piece of paper. Allocate 1 to heads and 0 to tails. Flip the coin and write down the result. Repeat this 256 times. Congratulations, you just created your own randomly generated Private Key. To start using this private key, you just need to create a public key. That's a little harder... but still possible with some complex mathematics. We'll save that for another book.

What makes Bitcoin unique is the ability for anyone to create their own Bitcoin public and private key without the need for any trusted third parties or banks. What's more, you could then memorize your private key and have bitcoin sent to your public key, and there is no way for anyone to know you are storing monetary value in your head. This is what makes Bitcoin incredibly resistant to seizure and theft. Your bitcoin does not exist in the physical realm. Instead, it is pure information and can be stored in our memory if needed.

Now that we have explored the public and private keys, let's look at how they are linked. This is known as the public and private key pair.

Public/Private Key Pair

For Bitcoin to be useful, we need both a public and private key pair. The public key allows us to receive bitcoin, and the private key enables us to spend our bitcoin.

To create this pair, we must start with the private key. As explained above in the "Fun Exercise," it is easy for anyone to create a private key if they prefer to tinker rather than rely on their wallet to do the heavy lifting. However, creating the public key is a little harder, as it is derived from the private key and involves some complex mathematics. This math is called Elliptic Curve Cryptography. This is far outside the scope of this book, but for simplicity, think of elliptic curve cryptography as a hash function of sorts. You start with a value, in this case, a private key. You then perform a series of complex equations, and out pops your public key– a private key goes in, and a public key comes out.

The beauty of the public/private key pair relationship is that through cryptography, we can easily confirm whether a transaction is legitimate or not. You could liken this to a credit card transaction. Say we want to purchase something in a store. Traditionally, we would have to sign the transaction receipt to verify we are indeed the credit card owner. The teller would then check our signature against the signature on the back of the card to confirm we are who we say we are. The teller would decline the transaction if we couldn't replicate the signature. This is similar to Bitcoin except for three caveats:

1. To forge the signature, you must guess the 64-character hexadecimal private key (or the 12 or 24-word seed phrase). That's a lot harder than forging a handwritten signature.
2. When we sign for a credit card transaction, we reveal our signature. In the case of Bitcoin, anyone can confirm the authenticity of the signature without revealing their private key through something known as a zero-knowledge proof.
3. In the example of the handwritten signature verification, we are relying on the discretion of the person comparing the two. With public/private keys, we rely on math and math alone. And Math doesn't lie.

Moreover, when we digitally sign a transaction to prove we're the owner of any funds, every node on the network automatically checks the transaction's legitimacy. If the signature does not match the public key, the network rejects the transaction.

Tying everything together, by deriving a public key from a private key, we can have people send us bitcoin without giving them access to our bitcoin. Knowing the public key does not unlock the ability to spend the balance held under the public key. Thinking back to our banking analogy, in this case, we have created a bank account number from our password, and these two are inextricably linked to one another using cryptography.

Got it? Not so fast... Our computer science friends discovered there might be a case where a computer may be able to crack this public/private key relationship. Hence, they added one more piece of protection to further encrypt the public keys, known as public addresses.

Public Addresses

Previously, we introduced the idea that if someone knows your public key, they can look up your bitcoin balance. Most people would agree that this is less than ideal. If Jack sends Jill 0.25BTC for a used car, Jill can look up the transaction details and see Jack's sending address. Jill can see Jack's entire history and balance in a few seconds. Surely Jack would want some privacy? We could just create a new public/private key pair each time we want to send/receive money. But this would be a nightmare. That's like opening a new bank account each time you wish to transact.

Here's where Public Addresses come in.

You now know that a public key is derived from a private key via complex mathematics. Similarly, public addresses are derived from our public key using another hash function. And, from our public key, we can generate as many public addresses as we like. To clarify further, here is an example.

Think of your home address as your Public Key. We don't want everyone globally to know our home address (public key) for security purposes. We, therefore, head over to the post office, show them our home address and open a PO Box (public address). This way, we can give out a PO Box address instead. Now imagine a world where every time we want to give out an address, we can easily and instantly open a PO Box address to receive any incoming mail. Since all of these PO Boxes are tied to our home address, our private key can access each of these PO Boxes. People can look inside the PO Box address they are given, but they can only see what is in that address. They cannot see all our mail (transactions and balances) as we have not given them our home address (public key).

And that is how the public address system works.

Don't worry if this went over your head. All the details around public address generation are managed by the bitcoin wallet (software) you use to store your keys.

It is common to see Public Addresses use a combination of upper and lower case letters alongside the numbers 0 through 9. Similar to base 16, which we introduced in the section on mining, this is another number system that reduces the number of characters needed and is known as base 58. Figure 2.43 shows the conversion from decimal to base 58. You will notice that some characters are omitted, such as the number 0 and the upper case O. This eliminates ambiguity and transposition errors.

Character	Value	Character	Value	Character	Value	Character	Value
1	0	G	15	X	30	n	45
2	1	H	16	Y	31	o	46
3	2	J	17	Z	32	p	47
4	3	K	18	a	33	q	48
5	4	L	19	b	34	r	49
6	5	M	20	c	35	s	50
7	6	N	21	d	36	t	51
8	7	P	22	e	37	u	52
9	8	Q	23	f	38	v	53
A	9	R	24	g	39	w	54
B	10	S	25	h	40	x	55
C	11	T	26	i	41	y	56
D	12	U	27	j	42	z	57
E	13	V	28	k	43		
F	14	W	29	m	44		

Figure 2.43: Base58 to Decimal Conversion Chart

Section Summary

Whoa, well done, that was some deep stuff! Public/Private key cryptography really is an engineering marvel that makes this technology possible. This form of cryptography is locking up and protecting billions and, at times, trillions of dollars worth of value and personal wealth. Although complex, it is needed to provide the utmost security. Next up, we will explore the ledger in detail. Get ready!

For further readings, we highly recommend:
"Public & Private Keys" - Arman the Parman
"Bitcoin Private Key" - Delton Rhodes
"Can I derive the private key from the public key?" - Prof Bill Buchanan

SECTION 5

The Ledger

Key Questions Answered:
What is a ledger?
Why does Bitcoin use a ledger?
How does Bitcoin solve the double-spend problem?

So far in this chapter, we discussed mining, the supply and public/ private key cryptography. Now we are going to explore where value is stored, the ledger.

What is the Bitcoin ledger?

The Bitcoin ledger is simply a list of pseudonymous transactions. It is pseudonymous in that it does not carry any personal information regarding the sender and receiver, only the transaction and address information. What is fascinating is that on this ledger, we can see the details of every bitcoin in existence and every movement of each bitcoin since its inception.

Through this chronological list of transactions, we can determine who owns what. As discussed earlier, the ledger is kept current by the miners and nodes continuously updating and monitoring it. Each time a new block is added to the blockchain, the ledger is updated to reflect any new transactions.

Facts (As of May 2022)

- Since Bitcoin's inception, there have been over <u>965,000,000</u>[29] addresses created and used.
- Currently, there are 40,276,163 bitcoin addresses with a balance greater than 0.
- Figure 2.51 is a chart from January 2021 that details how many addresses are in each cohort of wallet size. For example, there are 22,000,000 Shrimps (Wallets holding less than one bitcoin).

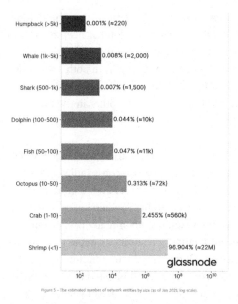

Figure 2.51: <u>*No. of Wallet Addresses By Size*</u>[30]

Why does Bitcoin use a ledger?

In general, there are two different ways to store value:

A Token (Physical): A tangible item of value that we can physically interact with and exchange.

A Ledger (Informational): A record of a sequence of events which allows us to determine who owns what.

In day-to-day life, we interact with both tokens and ledgers. For instance, when someone walks into a coffee shop and purchases a cookie, they could pay with cash (a physical token of value) or a credit card (an informational ledger of who owns what). If they choose cash, they hand over the cash to the teller and receive the cookie. They no longer have the cash, and the teller no longer has the cookie.

Alternatively, they could pay by credit card. If so, nothing physical is exchanged. Instead, a new transaction has been recorded on a ledger, debiting the purchaser and crediting the coffee shop, ultimately updating the location of value on the ledger. In both situations, value has been exchanged. However, in one instance, value has been exchanged in the physical realm (cash) and the other in the digital realm (credit card).

This example shows that for value to be exchanged in the digital realm, there has to be a ledger of records indicating who owns what. For this reason, tokens do not work in the digital realm. Without a ledger, there is no way to confirm ownership of value. Why? There is no way to prove the token has not already been spent, copied or duplicated, such as our picture of a sunset example in "The White Paper." I could quite easily tell my friend I am sending them the only copy of my sunset picture, only to have duplicated it before sending it. It is for this reason that digital scarcity is so hard to achieve. This is known as the double-spend problem. But, more on that in a second.

For now, what should be evident is that tokens work best at representing the exchange of value in the physical realm, whereas ledgers are the best means of recording the exchange of value in the digital realm. This explains why Bitcoin uses a ledger to record who owns what.

The double-spend problem

Due to a token's tangible nature, there is no need to track its history. Its value can only be in one place at any one time. Whereas, for digital information to exist in only one place, it must be deleted from the original owner once it has been moved to the new owner. This begs the question, how can one be certain digital money has not been copied and will not be re-spent?

For something to retain value in the digital realm, we must keep track of its movement. This is achieved by using a ledger– a detailed record of events. This allows us to determine the location of value, or in other words, who owns what at any time. However, it is also crucial that the order of events is accurate. This seems simple enough, doesn't it?

The Issue of Trust

A ledger is a list of transactions detailing the location of value. If we change the order or alter the record of transactions, we can change who owns what. Therefore, a ledger requires trust. We must be able to trust that the order of events is immutable– cannot be changed.

This may sound confusing, so let's build on the cookie example above. Let's say this person above stole the credit card. The owner of the card, while checking their card statement, notices this unknown transaction, calls up the credit card company and reports the transaction as fraudulent. In response, the credit card company reverses the transaction, changing the record of events on their centralized ledger. It is as if the event never happened, except the coffee shop is now down a cookie and has nothing to show for it.

Now, what if you were the coffee shop? How would you feel? It is not your fault that someone stole a credit card and purchased something in your shop.

If the thief had stolen a wallet, paying for the cookie with cash, there would be no way to reverse the transaction as there would be no reversible ledger record. Therefore, we can conclude that in the physical realm, the transaction is final. There is no need for trust.

However, in the digital realm, the transaction is not final. Since the transaction is just an event recorded on a ledger, the record can be altered, changed, or reversed if a central entity controls this ledger. Not good!

What have we learnt? Centralized systems can rewrite their version of history.

So, although we have solved the double-spend problem through the use of a ledger, when we have to rely on third parties to manage the ledger, we are still faced with the issue of needing to trust those centralized entities to determine and maintain the true state of the ledger.

Back to the drawing board...

How can we prevent double-spending or someone rewriting history in a decentralized manner so we don't need to trust anyone? It's harder than it looks, although, with everything we have covered so far, we now have all the pieces to the puzzle!

How does Bitcoin solve the double-spend problem?

Without going back over too much ground, let's piece together how Bitcoin achieves trustless decentralization while at the same time removing the potential for a double-spend.

Public/Private Key Cryptography
Through the use of public/private key cryptography, only the owner of the bitcoin can sign for and send transactions. This prevents miners from altering transactions to their benefit. If they were to attempt to alter the transaction, it would no longer be valid and would be dismissed by the network of nodes.

Blockchain
Through linking together blocks via the "Previous Block Hash" and creating a blockchain, two things are achieved:

Transaction Finality
If a nefarious miner decides to go back and alter a block in the chain, they'd have to mine the altered block, and subsequent blocks, faster than the entire network is mining blocks until their chain is longer than the main chain. This means the bad actor would have to expend the equivalent energy it took the entire network of miners to build the original blockchain. Therefore, it is essentially impossible for any miner to go back and alter the blockchain due to the time, energy, cost and challenge of finding enough hardware to do so.

For this reason, Bitcoin is described as having transaction finality, a.k.a immutability. Once a transaction has been added to a block and appended to the blockchain, it is final as it's near impossible to reverse/alter, unlike our centralized credit card example above.

Chronological Order

Order is a necessity when keeping a ledger of transactions. We know the order of transactions via the sequence of blocks. By linking one block to the next, we have a verifiable chronological record of history. This, combined with transaction finality, means we have an indisputable and immutable history of events.

Miners and Nodes

As our transaction is processed by a random miner in the network and is then verified by every node on the network, we do not have to put any trust in any single entity. We have a trustless, decentralized system. Everyone in the network keeps everyone else honest. As a miner, when you are the lucky one appending your block to the blockchain, there is no incentive to try to alter or cheat the rest of the Bitcoin network, as your changes will be disregarded, and you will lose the block reward.

Section Summary

Piecing all the above together, we have a finished puzzle of how Bitcoin solves the double-spend problem. Through the use of distributed ledgers, blockchain technology, miners, nodes and public/private key cryptography, for the first time in history, we have a decentralized, chronological, constantly audited and immutable record of who owns what.

For further readings, we highly recommend:
"Bitcoin is Time" - Dergigi

SECTION 6

UTXOs & Transaction Fees

Key Questions Answered:
What is a UTXO?
What are transaction fees?
Why do transaction fees increase when more people transact?
What do transaction fees have to do with UTXOs?

So far, we have thrown a lot at you, keys, blocks, hashing... all heavy stuff. But, there are two more important subjects we want to touch on before moving on to chapter three. These are Unspent Transaction Outputs, UTXOs for short, and transaction fees.

What is a UTXO?

As discussed previously, the Bitcoin ledger contains a chronological list of every transaction since inception. This allows us to determine who owns what. However, unlike a traditional ledger with credits and debits, where our wallet balance is the sum total of all credits and debits, Bitcoin uses something called a UTXO model. Our wallet balance is the sum total of all unspent transaction outputs we have received but have yet to spend. This may sound confusing, so let's break this down.

Any time a bitcoin transaction occurs, it uses UTXOs to track ownership and balances.

Suppose we open our traditional physical wallet, and inside is a $5 bill and a $10 bill– money we have received at some point but have not yet spent. These two bills can be thought of as two unspent transaction outputs. Combined, these UTXOs give our wallet a total balance of $15.

Every Bitcoin transaction is made up of inputs and outputs. These Inputs consume existing UTXOs, while outputs create new UTXOs.

Let's say we want to purchase a burger for $11. Clearly, we do not have the exact change for this burger as we only have one $5 and one $10 bill. The transaction would, therefore, consist of the inputs, a $5 bill and a $10 bill. These UTXOs will now be consumed, and we will be given outputs in return. The restaurant receives a new $11 bill, and we receive a new $4 bill. Our wallet balance now contains a new UTXO of $4, and the restaurant contains a UTXO of $11.

What's important to note is that the total inputs have to equal the outputs, and UTXOs cannot be broken down into smaller denominations. They have to be consumed in full, just like with dollar bills. We can't just chop up our $5 bill into a $4 and $1 bill, giving the restaurant one $10 and one $1 bill, keeping $4 for ourselves. We have to consume our two UTXOs of $5 and $10, creating two new UTXOs of $11 for the restaurant and $4 for ourselves.

What Are Transaction Fees?

To transact on the Bitcoin network, we must pay transaction fees. These fees compensate the miners for expending energy to process our transactions.

However, unlike PayPal, which charges a flat fee of 2.9%, Bitcoin transaction fees may vary based on the network congestion and the digital size of the transaction (as opposed to the amount of value it represents).

The more people using the network, the more costly it is to transact and vice versa. You could liken this to Christmas shopping. If we wait until Christmas eve to shop, we'll have to face congested roads and stores, increasing the time and energy we have to expend to complete our shopping. On the flip side, if we shop outside of the holiday season, the roads and stores are quieter, leading to reduced time and energy consumption.

Additionally, when we send a bitcoin transaction, we can usually select how much of a fee we wish to pay. The more we pay, the faster our transaction will be processed.

If we desperately need to send 500,000 satoshis across the globe to El Salvador, we can increase our transaction fee to better our chances of it being included in the next block.

Alternatively, we can set a low transaction fee if we're not in a rush. It may just take a while for our transaction to be processed, as we'll be waiting for network demand to decline to where our transaction fee is acceptable. This is because miners often prioritize transactions with higher fees to maximize revenue. The higher the fee, the higher the priority given.

This raises the question, why do transaction fees increase when more people transact?

Simply put, each block has a maximum size, or in other words, limited space for transactions.

Bitcoin transaction fees are charged in sats per virtual byte– the more space a transaction takes up, the higher the fee. This is a powerful concept to understand. The size of transactions varies based on the complexity of the transaction. This includes things like the number of inputs (UTXOs) that make up a transaction.

This fee structure differs from traditional payment rails, which usually charge a percentage fee– the more value you send, the higher the fee. Whereas with Bitcoin, the transaction fee for sending 10,000 bitcoin may be the same as sending 0.00001 bitcoin.

What's more, if the transaction fee is still too much, you can use technology built on top of Bitcoin, such as Lightning, for almost instantaneous transaction time and fractions-of-a-cent, if not zero, transaction fees.

What do transaction fees have to do with UTXOs?

If you recall above, total UTXO inputs must equal the UTXO outputs. When we send a bitcoin transaction, we must have a sufficient total balance held within the UTXOs in our wallet to cover the transaction + the transaction fee.

Suppose we want to buy a cup of coffee for 4000 sats, and our wallet tells us it's currently 100 sats for the transaction fee. For us to be able to proceed with the transaction, we must have a minimum of 4100 sats in our UTXOs.

Lucky for us, we checked our wallet, and we have a balance of 5300 sats, made up of one UTXO for 1000 sats, one for 2000 sats and one for 2300 sats.

If we went ahead with the transaction, the input for the transaction would look like this:
1. UTXO for 2000 sats
2. UTXO for 2300 sats

And the output for the transaction would look like this:
1. A new UTXO for 4000 sats to pay for the coffee.
2. A new UTXO which includes our 100 sat transaction fee + the block subsidy and all the other transaction fees in which the transaction was confirmed.

A new UTXO for 200 sats that we received back, which is the change from our original 4300 (2000 + 2300) sats minus the 4000 sat coffee, and 100 sat transaction fee.

Notice how we never used our UTXO for 1000 sats? This is because there was no need to include it in the transaction. Our UTXOs for 2000 and 2300 covered the cost of our coffee and the transaction fee.

When we use cash, we choose the bills we'd like to use. Whereas with Bitcoin, our wallet software decides which UTXOs are used in a transaction. With the software designed to optimize the use of our UTXOs for efficient data management. This way, our wallet will use the least amount of UTXOs to conserve data usage since fees are charged based on data usage, not the transaction amount.

If you want to get fancy, many wallets offer UTXO user management these days. You can decide which UTXOs to use in a transaction.

Section Summary

With chapter two under our belt, we have now explored the underlying processes that make the Bitcoin network the unique technology it is. In the next chapter, we will move away from the technicals and dive into the participants involved in bringing Bitcoin to life.

CHAPTER 3

The Various Ways To Interact with Bitcoin

"in the future, one of the milestones by which you measure your financial success will be not just now many zeroes you can add to your net worth, but whether you can structure your affairs in a way that enables you to realize full individual autonomy and independence." - James Dale Davidson, The Sovereign Individual

SECTION 1

Miners

Key Questions Answered:
What is Proof of Work?
What are miners?
Can we measure the computational effort of all Bitcoin miners?

Now that we have a deeper understanding of Bitcoin Mining from chapter two let's look at the people, organizations and hardware that perform the act of bitcoin mining. But first, let's solidify some mining terminology and introduce the concept of Proof of Work.

What is Proof of Work?

Proof of Work (PoW) is the name given to the process by which miners secure the Bitcoin blockchain. As you will recall, miners expend energy hashing in an attempt to get their "Block Hash" below the target value.

The first miner to do so can simply show that their "Block Hash" is below the target value, which is "Proof" that a certain amount of computational effort or "Work" has been completed. Why is this proof? There is no other possible way to get the "Block Hash" below the target value than expending energy through the random guessing game of hashing. Hence the term, Proof of Work.

"But why can we rely on work in the first place? The answer is threefold. We can rely on it because computation requires work, work requires time, and the work in question—guessing random numbers—can not be done efficiently." - Gigi

What are miners?
These days, miners are computers that specialize in hashing. In the early days of Bitcoin, it was possible to mine bitcoin with a standard PC. However, as the price of bitcoin grew, so did the monetary incentives behind mining. As a result of this, and due to the increased processing power of newer machines, miners' computational output and efficiency increased, and the processing chips miners used became more and more specialized.

In 2013, we saw the introduction of Application Specific Integrated Circuits (ASICs). These contraptions are explicitly designed for hashing bitcoin and significantly increase efficiency. At this moment, it became virtually impossible for the little guy to compete using an at-home computer.

Can we measure the computational effort of all Bitcoin miners?
The rate at which the network of miners collectively hashes is called the hash rate[32]. Bitcoin's hash rate is currently[33] 221.74 million TH/s (terrahashes per second), and this has been increasing steadily since its inception. With a terrahash being 1,000,000,000,000 hashes, that means all of the miners globally are currently hashing 221,740,000,000,000,000,000 times per second. As more miners com-

pete to validate transactions, the network becomes ever more secure. Therefore, we can view the hash rate as a measure of security. The higher the hash rate, the more secure the Bitcoin network is and the less vulnerable it is to attack.

Figure 3.11: *A Bitcoin Miner[31]*

Fun Fact: Many bitcoiners tend to check metrics such as Bitcoin hash rate and indicators of global adoption as far more accurate indicators of Bitcoin's increasing value than its price on any given day.

So who runs these miners?

A wide variety of companies and individuals alike choose to partake in Bitcoin mining. Different types of mining include:

Home mining - When an individual chooses to run mining equipment within their home. Fun fact: These days, people are finding ways to use the heat from the miners to heat their homes, replacing traditional heating systems.

Mining pools - A conglomerate of individuals who proportionately split mining proceeds based on the hash rate they've contributed.

Hosted mining/Co-located mining - When individuals or companies choose to let a hosted mining facility host their mining hardware. The individual owns the machine but pays a fee to the mining facility. Why? Mining facilities typically have access to cheap energy.

Commercial mining - When smaller companies make use of unused office space, commercial units or data centers, converting them into mining operations.

Industrial mining - When large-scale mining operations use repurposed industrial facilities or purpose-built facilities.

Figure 3.12: An Industrial Bitcoin Mining Operation[34]

Although a significant proportion of the overall hash rate is from large mining companies, it is still common for individuals to participate in mining pools and hosted mining.

Is it profitable to mine bitcoin?

The answer to this question is, it depends. A lot of variables need to be considered when it comes to mining bitcoin, most of which fall outside the scope of this book. In saying that, under the right conditions and circumstances, mining can be very profitable since if it weren't, nobody would do it. However, the critical factor to consider is input energy costs. If you lack access to a cheap energy source, Bitcoin mining will most likely be uneconomical.

> **Fun Fact:** Bitcoin has many incentives built into it. One of these is the potential to make money mining bitcoin if you have access to cheap input energy. This has led to a quickly developing industry connecting bitcoin mining equipment to 'stranded' forms of energy (energy that has no other use). This is changing the economics of the energy industry and also encouraging the use of 'green' energy.

Why can't we just add more computers and find all the bitcoin?

Initially, when more miners come online and the network's hash rate increases, blocks are solved more quickly than the target time of 10mins. However, as mentioned previously, for every 2016 blocks, the Bitcoin Protocol assesses the average time taken per block and adjusts the difficulty accordingly– if blocks were being mined faster than 10 minutes, the difficulty increases and vice versa.

In May 2021, the Chinese government banned Proof of Work mining due to its perceived impact on the energy grid. A mass exodus of Chinese-based miners ensued. Mining operations shut down almost over-night and fled China in search of mining-friendly jurisdictions. This sudden drop in active miners immediately caused a decline in the hash rate and increased time between each block. However, this increase in the block time only lasted two weeks. Just as it is programmed to do, after 2016 blocks, the protocol adjusted difficulty making it easier to mine Bitcoin and the block time returned to ~10mins.

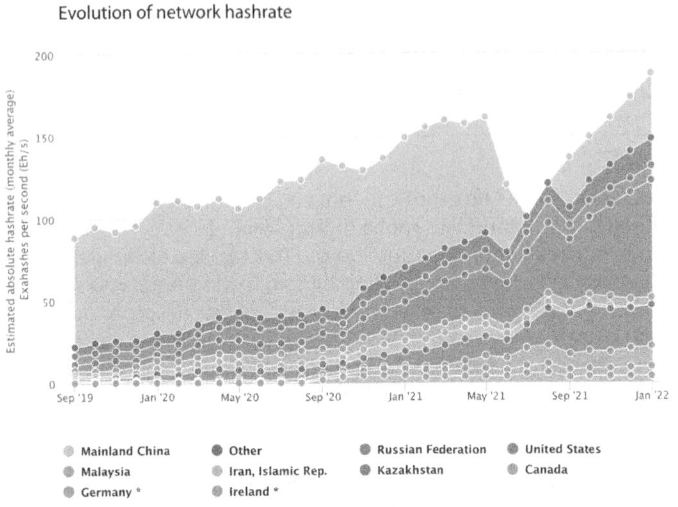

Figure 3.13: *Evolution of Network Hashrate*[35]

This event was one of the greatest tests of the resiliency of the Bitcoin network. The hash rate of Bitcoin saw a 50%+ decline, yet the func-tionality of Bitcoin never skipped a beat! Over time, the lost hash rate returned, and the Bitcoin Protocol continued to adjust its difficulty every 2016 blocks to maintain that steady, predictable release rate.

Section Summary

With the mining industry rapidly evolving and expanding, what works one day, may not work the next. Case in point, in Bitcoin's early years, anyone could mine bitcoin successfully on their home PC. Unfortunately, that is no longer the case.

However, that is not to say we don't have options...

For the Bitcoin enthusiast, this article has hopefully demonstrated not only the resilience of the miner network but the many ways to get involved in mining. We could purchase a miner, contribute to a mining pool, pay for hosted mining, etc. That said, whether your desired path to mining is profitable is another question.

Now, let's look at one of the other integral parts of the network... the nodes.

For further readings, we highly recommend:
"Bitcoin Mining" - NYDIG

SECTION 2

Nodes, Developers & Consensus

Key Questions Answered:
What are nodes?
Who can run a node?
Do I need to run a node?
How are changes made to Bitcoin?

Nodes are one of the most important aspects of the Bitcoin network. They are really the most fundamental element of what makes Bitcoin so hard to break, co-opt, control or coerce.

Let's dive in.

What are nodes?

Nodes, in addition to the miners, are what make Bitcoin decentralized and maintain its integrity.

What's more, it is the role of the nodes to enforce and decide on the network rules. If you don't play by the rules, your transaction may be denied, or as a miner, your block rejected.

It is the nodes that keep the Bitcoin network honest. They're continuously checking in with one another to ensure their version of the blockchain matches that of the majority.

You may still be wondering, "I get what they do, but what is a node?"

Simply put, a node is a computer that runs the Bitcoin software. Running this software means the node downloads and maintains an up-to-date copy of both the entire Bitcoin blockchain and the rule set.

There are many iterations of the Bitcoin Software, with Bitcoin Core[36] being one of the more popular examples.

Who can run a node?

Absolutely anyone. As long as you have access to a basic computer, sufficient hard drive capacity and an internet connection, you can run a node. That means whether you have a standard PC, Laptop, Macbook, Windows or Linux Machine, running a node is easily accessible.

Alternatively, you can build your own dedicated node using a hard drive, Raspberry Pi (a miniature credit card-sized computer) and an internet connection. This enables you to separate your node from your standard computer.

Figures 3.21 and 3.22 are two examples of nodes. The first is a pre-built, ready-to-go Raspberry Pi node (in a nice case) by a company called Umbrel and the second is a homemade node, also a Raspberry

Pi, built by one of the great Bitcoin educators in the space, Arman the Parman.

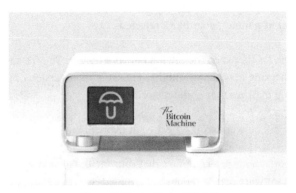

Figure 3.21: An Umbrel Node[37]

Figure 3.22: Raspberry Pi Node[38]

And in figure 3.23 is a screenshot of the Umbrel node in action.

Figure 3.23: Umbrel Node Software

Why would you run a node?

There are a number of reasons people choose to run a node. Those include:

1. **Participate in the network:** Running a node allows you to participate in the first true peer-to-peer, digitally native, cash-like payments system. It will enable you to vote on the changes you believe should be implemented.
2. **Decentralization:** By running a node, you are contributing to the decentralization of the Bitcoin blockchain. The more people that run a node, the more distributed the Bitcoin ledger.
3. **Analyze:** By running a node, you have access to every Bitcoin transaction that has ever taken place. If desired, this allows you to analyze the movement of bitcoin to and from wallets and the flow of capital into and out of the network.
4. **Management:** Most node software offers tools which assist you in managing your keys, payments, transactions and UTXOs.

5. **Verification:** Operating your own node allows you to monitor your own transactions, ensuring your bitcoin are indeed your bitcoin. This illustrates a central principle of Bitcoin: "Don't trust, verify."

Let's expand a little on a few of these thoughts.

Firstly, by running a node, you are contributing to the decentralization of the Bitcoin Blockchain. Every node connected to the network makes it that little bit harder for bad actors to impact the functionality of Bitcoin.

Why? Bitcoin is not static. As a node, you have a say in what new rules and changes are implemented. This decision is made through consensus. If only a few nodes made up the Bitcoin network, someone could easily set up a handful of new nodes, obtaining majority voting power. This may allow them to implement undesirable changes to the Bitcoin code.

On the flip side, having a decentralized distributed network with thousands of geographically dispersed nodes makes it practically impossible to create undesirable changes without consensus.

In saying that, if the community cannot agree on a change, there is a mechanism known as a hard fork. This will separate the two opposing sides into separate assets, preserving the original values of Bitcoin prior to any undesirable changes. However, as we will soon explain in more depth, the community tries to avoid hard forks as they usually lead to fracturing within the community.

But more on this in a second.

Secondly, one of the major attractions of running a node is that you can personally verify all Bitcoin transactions, including your own.

Typically, if you hold bitcoin on an exchange or in a third-party wallet (we explain these in the next section), you rely on that third-party's node to search the blockchain, find your addresses and tally up your account balances. Not only do you give up privacy regarding your account balances, but you also have to trust that the balance the third party displays is correct. By running a node, you can personally verify your transactions and account balance without giving up privacy.

Do I need to run a node?

What makes Bitcoin so powerful is that the decision to run a node is up to the user.

In saying that, running a node isn't for everyone. We understand that, depending on the approach, running a node can involve technical skills that fall outside some people's desire or capability. Even if you decide against running a node, you can still participate in the bitcoin network, buy bitcoin, custody bitcoin, interact with the blockchain and verify transactions. You just forfeit the ability to participate in consensus and give up privacy when verifying transactions.

You may still be wondering, what does participating in consensus mean?

As mentioned above, Bitcoin is not static. The core Bitcoin protocol has stayed true to its original intent. There has always been only 21 million bitcoin, a four-year halving cycle, a difficulty adjustment regulating the supply of bitcoin to the market, etc. However, as the technology surrounding privacy, security and cryptography is always advancing, Bitcoin needs a way to keep up, ensuring improvements are implemented and vulnerabilities to the protocol can be addressed.

With this in mind, there is an active community of Bitcoin developers that are constantly working on improving the Bitcoin protocol.

How are changes to Bitcoin proposed and made?

The Bitcoin community uses something called the BIP system, which stands for the Bitcoin Improvement Proposal. There are generally four stages when it comes to changing the Bitcoin protocol:

1. A BIP is put forth by a developer(s) or participants who feel a change or improvement to the Bitcoin code is warranted. Within a BIP, you'll find the developer's proposed update, justification and other relevant information (All previous and current BIPs can be found on GitHub[39], a hosting site for shared software development).

2. After a BIP has been proposed and before it is put forward for implementation, it will be rigorously debated, and other developers will review, pick apart, interrogate and try to find faults in the code. This can take months, if not years, to go through.

3. Once the majority of developers agree upon a BIP, we see another level of consensus called "signalling of support." Miners signal their intention to support these changes by including messages of support within the blocks they mine (i.e. recently, there was an upgrade to improve the privacy and efficiency of the network called Taproot. For Taproot to be approved, 90% of miners had to signal their support)

4. When the minimum predefined support signalling level is reached, the decision is passed over to the nodes. It is the nodes who decide whether to adopt the newly proposed changes or not. If they decide to adopt the changes, they simply run the newest version of the code. Alternatively, they stick with their current code version if they want to reject the changes.

But what if the nodes can't come to a consensus?

As briefly discussed above, when the nodes don't agree to changes, there are two potential paths forward, depending on the changes being proposed:

Soft Forks

Usually, upgrades to bitcoin are attempted through something known as a soft fork. This simply means that when a change is proposed, it is backwards compatible with older software versions. In other words, nodes that might not agree, or have yet to upgrade their software, are still compatible with the new version proposed. When a soft fork takes place, there is no interruption to the "tick-tock-next-block" functionality of Bitcoin.

A soft fork is the desired path when proposing changes to the Bitcoin protocol due to its backwards compatibility with previous instances of the software.

Hard Forks

A hard fork, on the other hand, is a radical change to the protocol whereby the change is not backwards compatible. All nodes or users must upgrade to the latest version of the protocol software to continue using the protocol.

A hard fork ensues when there is a lack of consensus, as the nodes cannot agree on whether to implement a BIP. As a result, two blockchains are formed, one with the original protocol and one with the new protocol. The minority blockchain becomes a new asset.

With both blockchains operating as separate assets, it is up to the free market as to which blockchain reigns supreme. But more on that in a second...

Due to the conflict and community fracturing during a hard fork, backwards-compatible soft forks are the preferred upgrade option.

However, sometimes a hard fork is the only option.

One of the more contentious hard forks was during an event known as the Block Size Wars.

Long story short, a handful of influential individuals, exchanges, developers and mining companies proposed a change to increase the number of transactions that can be processed per block. This would be achieved by increasing the size of a Bitcoin block. Hence, the name Blocksize Wars. Even though discussions were had, the community could not reach a consensus. A hard fork ensued, and we saw the emergence of Bitcoin Cash (BCH) alongside Bitcoin.

In the end, Bitcoin, as we know it today, proved to be the superior asset, continuing its meteoric rise in market cap, price and network adoption, while Bitcoin Cash was slowly left behind.

What is interesting about hard forks is that if you were an owner of the token before the hard fork, post-hard fork, you would now own both tokens. In this instance, Bitcoin and BCH. If you do not align with the changes made by BCH, you could sell your BCH tokens and invest the proceeds back into Bitcoin, or vice versa. It is now up to the free market to decide which protocol is superior.

You could liken a soft fork to adding a new word to a language. You may not understand this new word, but you still speak the same language. Therefore, not learning this new word (upgrading your software) doesn't interrupt your ability to communicate with others who speak the same language.

A hard fork, on the other hand, is like creating a completely new language. If your node adopts this new language, it can no longer communicate with nodes running the original language.

Section Summary

We feel it is essential to understand the tradeoffs between running a node and relying on others, but ultimately, the decision on whether to run a node is up to you. That said, if you support Bitcoin as a savings or investment vehicle, one of the best things you can do as an individual is to run a node and further distribute the Bitcoin network.

This section was most likely a heavy one. However, we cannot stress the importance of the nodes enough. It is through the nodes and their consensus mechanism that we can update Bitcoin while simultaneously preventing centralized entities from wandering in and making changes to the protocol without consensus from the community– something we have lost in traditional banking.

Without the many thousands of nodes, we wouldn't have the resilient and secure network and asset that is Bitcoin. Instead, we would have something that was co-opted and centrally controlled a long time ago.

SECTION 3

On-Chain & Off-Chain

Key Questions Answered:
Why is Bitcoin limited in the number of transactions it can pro-
cess per second?
What do on-chain and off-chain mean?

On-chain and off-chain are terms that help describe some of the innovations in, around and on top of Bitcoin. We need to set the scene here
to illustrate why these different chains are essential.

It may sound counter-intuitive, but the Bitcoin network is very delib-
erate in its slow and steady approach to development and scalability.
The reason for this is to prioritize security and decentralization.

In doing so, however, Bitcoin's usability and scalability have often
been criticized.

Generally, the critics fail to realize that innovative usability and scalability solutions are already available and in use, and more continue to emerge.

Being that most of this innovation is off-chain, in order to preserve security and decentralization, there is often some confusion:

- Why are there on-chain and off-chain transactions?
- Why can't I locate my bitcoin transaction on-chain?
- Am I still sending bitcoin if I am transacting off-chain?

As we will see, these questions tend to stem from a misunderstanding of the various ways to transact using bitcoin. With that said, let's explore the idea behind "Block Space," as this will lay the groundwork for understanding on-chain and off-chain transactions.

Block Space

Each block on the Bitcoin base chain has a maximum size (around one megabyte in size). However, with each block being limited in size, there is an upper limit to how many transactions Bitcoin can process per second on the base layer. At this time, that limit sits around seven transactions per second (tps).

You may be wondering, "how can Bitcoin possibly compete with networks such as Visa or Mastercard that transact at 1,700 tps?"[40]

The answer is simple. It is not competing with them.

Comparing Bitcoin to Visa or Mastercard is like comparing an international container ship to a checkout at a local hardware store.

The container ship is intended for infrequent bulk transactions, whereas a checkout is built around high-frequency, small transactions. Although both move goods, comparing them is like comparing apples to oranges.

With this in mind, Bitcoin offers trustless, permissionless transactions with final settlement, while Visa and Mastercard provide convenience and ease of use. However, that is not to say Bitcoin doesn't offer these things too. It just doesn't try to achieve them on the base chain or base layer as it's commonly known.

Let's explore what this means...

Layers

When inspecting any monetary system, there are often different methods, or layers, of transacting, with each method offering various benefits to the user.

The layers of transacting in our current monetary system include:

Layer One

This layer often involves high-value transactions with low throughput, meaning it is limited in how many transactions can be processed per second.

Examples of layer one transactions in our traditional monetary system include bank wire transfers and Fed Wire interbank transfers. Both are used for high-value transactions; however, they tend to be slow and costly, with wire transfer fees anywhere from $10 to $50 and processing times often taking many days.

Although layer one transactions can be incredibly secure and reliable, layer one methods of transacting fall short in their ability to meet the needs of consumers looking to transact in smaller denominations or for timely, cost-effective transactions.

Layer Two

This layer often involves low-value transactions with high through-put, meaning many transactions can be processed per second. It also features high-speed transactions, taking only a few seconds, as well as offering lower fees, generally around 1-3% of the transaction value.

Examples of layer two transactions in our traditional monetary system include credit and debit card payments and gift card transactions, to name a couple.

Where does Bitcoin fit into layer one and layer two transactions?

Bitcoin can be thought of as a great alternative to layer one. Although it may not be able to match the speed of a layer two Visa payment, Bitcoin can be used to transfer upwards of $\underline{\$1,000,000,000}$[41] at a fraction of the speed and cost of traditional layer one methods. In addition, and more importantly, it does so in a permissionless and trustless manner, without the need for intermediaries.

However, that is not to say Bitcoin cannot compete with layer two transaction methods.

Just like our traditional monetary system has layer one and two trans-actions, so does Bitcoin.

If you're looking for a reasonably quick (but not instant), cost-effective and secure way of sending a large amount of money, then Bitcoin is your best bet. Whereas, if you're looking to transact near-instanta-neously and for fractions of a cent, then you will want to direct your attention to some of the technologies built on top of Bitcoin. These can be thought of as layer two methods of transacting and include innova-tions such as Lightning.

On-chain & Off-chain

Any Bitcoin transaction processed over the base layer/layer one is classified as an on-chain transaction. This means you can locate the transaction and confirm whether and when it was processed in the Bitcoin block explorer (history of all transactions).

If, however, we transact using a layer two solution, although we are still sending and receiving bitcoin, it is no longer classified as "on-chain." If we attempt to search for our transaction in the block explorer, our transaction would be nowhere to be found. We would therefore say that the transaction is "off-chain."

Why would you transact off-chain?

As mentioned above, transacting off-chain or using layer two solutions often significantly reduces the transaction fees and greatly increases the speed of the transaction, albeit with reduced security.

Let's look at a hypothetical example...

Dan and Josh work, adventure, hang out together and are both passionate Bitcoiners. During a typical week, Dan may pay for gas while Josh will grab food and coffee. With this in mind, there are two approaches they could take to settle up with one another:

1. They could settle up after each transaction. Let's assume for this example that the fee for transacting on-chain is $1 and that Dan and Josh share three transactions per week. That means that after a month of settling up after each transaction, Dan and Josh will have spent $12 on transaction fees (4 weeks x 3 transactions per week).

2. Alternatively, they could keep a tab on how much each has spent

and settle up at the end of the month. By keeping a tab, Dan and Josh know how much was spent by whom, but more importantly, they don't have to incur the transaction fee after each transaction. Instead, they settle once at the end of the month for a total of $1 in fees.

In both situations, Dan and Josh are made whole. However, in the second situation, Dan and Josh save $11 in fees by using an ongoing tab to track each other's balance rather than settling up after each transaction. Additionally, they maintained greater privacy in their spending since their transactions were not recorded on-chain.

Although the technology may vary between different off-chain transaction methods, the idea is the same. Rather than transacting on-chain for each transaction, there is an off-chain ledger of record which records who owns what. And when a user wants to head back to the main chain, the balance is settled through a final on-chain transaction. This makes off-chain transacting not only faster but significantly cheaper.

Fun Fact: Lightning is currently the most popular of the layer two solutions. So much so that when El Salvador declared Bitcoin to be legal tender, they chose the Lightning Network for the day-to-day transactions of the populous.

Unsure whether to use on-chain or off-chain? Here is a handful of scenarios and the ideal method of transacting, assuming the transacting party accepts bitcoin:

- Buying a coffee - Off-chain (Layer 2)
- Transferring upwards of a few thousand dollars - On-chain (Layer 1)

- Ensuring a non-immediate payment gets to its destination with final settlement - On-chain
- Paying for dinner at a restaurant - Off-chain
- Purchasing a car - On-chain
- Purchasing something from an online marketplace - Off-chain
- A payment is significant enough to warrant spending the Bitcoin transaction fee of $0.70 to $2 - On-chain
- Sending $100 back home to your family - Off-chain
- Transferring your savings to cold storage - On-chain

To conclude, people often incorrectly compare Bitcoin to Visa, failing to realize that off-chain technologies such as lightning exist which have drastically increased Bitcoin's scalability.

As should now be evident, comparing Bitcoin to Visa is like comparing a Ferrari to a bus. They both serve different purposes.

Next time you hear someone criticize Bitcoin's speed, you're now ready to explain the misunderstanding.

For further readings, we highly recommend:
"Layered Money" - Nik Bhatia
"Visa and Lightning, how do they compare?" - Nicolas Burtley

SECTION 4

The Mempool

Key Questions Answered:
What is the Mempool?

Throughout this book, we have mentioned the mempool on multiple occasions. For many, this may have gone in one ear and out the other, but for the curious ones, we wanted to give a little more information on what this mempool is and what you can do with it.

Let's dive in...

The memory pool, mempool for short, is the limbo state where unconfirmed transactions sit after they have been initiated but before they have been confirmed and added to the blockchain.

We can view the mempool block explorer in action at www.mempool. space or here https://bits.monospace.live/

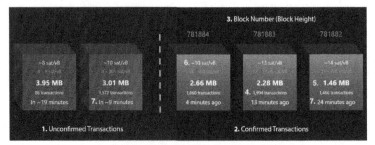

Figure 3.41: The Mempool

At first glance, the mempool can be a little confusing and so here is a breakdown:

(1.) Unconfirmed Transactions
All the transactions to the left of the white dotted line are unconfirmed.

What does this mean? If you were waiting to receive 0.001 BTC from a friend, your wallet would most likely pick up the transaction the moment it is initiated. However, until the transaction is processed and confirmed, it will sit in the mempool as an unconfirmed transaction. As a result, you will not have access to these funds until it is confirmed.

(2.) Confirmed Transactions
All the blocks and their transactions to the right of the white dotted line are confirmed.

These transactions are essentially irreversible. However, for cautionary reasons, most exchanges will wait for six blocks before allowing users to access their funds.

Why do they wait for six blocks? If you recall, from "Blockchain, Hashing & Mining," miners build off the longest chain. That means in the rare occurrence that two blocks are mined at once, there can be confusion as to which chain is the longest. In this scenario, there is a chain split. Some miners build on one chain while the remainder is on the other. This split will continue until one chain is clearly longer than the other. At that point, the miners on the shorter chain abandon their blocks, and their processed transactions from the split onwards are added back into the mempool (these discarded blocks are known as orphan blocks). This reverses the status of these transactions from confirmed to unconfirmed.

For this reason, we say Bitcoin is essentially irreversible, as, in certain scenarios, there is a slim possibility for newly confirmed transactions to be reversed shortly after they are confirmed.

(3.) The Block Height
The block height of a particular block indicates the number of blocks preceding that block in the blockchain. Another way to think of it is the number of blocks since Bitcoin's inception. For instance, a block height of 781,884 would mean it is the 781,884th block since Bitcoin began.

(4.) Transaction Count
As we are sure you've guessed, the transaction count is the total number of transactions inside a specific block. For instance, in block 781,883, there were 1,994 transactions.

(5.) Block Size
As there is a variance in the size of Bitcoin transactions (depending on the complexity of the transaction), and transaction volume, not every block is identical in size.

Although each block "technically" has an upper bound of 1mb in size, if one block contains more complex transactions or is confirmed during a period of increased transaction volume, it'll most likely be

larger than a block processed during a period of lesser use.
We say "technically," a block has an upper bound. However, due to
an upgrade called SegWit, the concept of block size was replaced with
block weight, so, in practice, blocks can be slightly larger than 1MB, as
shown above with block 781,882.

Moreover, mempool.space goes one step further and colours the
blocks. This indicates how full a block is, i.e. block 735,797 is 521.53
kB in size and only partially coloured. This tells us that there was still
significant space in that block for more transactions.

(6.) Average Transaction Fee

With the fees for bitcoin transactions varying, each block indicates the
average fee paid by all the transactions within the block. For example,
in block 781,884, we see ~10 sats/vB. This tells us it costs 10 satoshis
(0.00000010 bitcoin) per virtual byte. If a transaction were 200 virtual
bytes in size, it would cost 200 x 10 = 2,000 satoshis or roughly $1 at
today's prices.

(7.) Transaction Time

Transaction time shows us either when the block was processed if the
block is to the right of the white dotted line or an estimation of when
the block will be processed when the block is to the left of the dotted
line.

A transaction time of 24 minutes in block 781,882 simply tells us that
it has been 24 minutes since the block was processed. Remember,
blocks are released every 10 minutes on average, sometimes they are
slower, and sometimes they are quicker.

And that is the mempool...

Section Summary

If you're curious to look under the hood of the Bitcoin blockchain, then the mempool is the best place to start. Regardless of whether you own Bitcoin or not, the mempool is where anyone can see the blocks and transactions being processed in real time.

What's more, if you really want to get your hands dirty, you can dive into each of these blocks and start following the trail of bitcoin from one account to another. Although, that's for another book.

Hopefully, this intimidating website with colours, numbers and far too much information now makes a little more sense.

In the next couple of sections, it is time to explore the available options for purchasing and securely storing Bitcoin.

SECTION 5

Acquiring bitcoin

Key Questions Answered:
What are the three primary ways to acquire bitcoin?

Now that we have dug into the mysterious founder, Satoshi and explored the ins and outs of the Bitcoin network and examined the various players involved. It is time to move on from the theory and into the practical applications of Bitcoin.

To start, let's answer arguably the most important question:

How do I acquire bitcoin?

Unlike many other assets, one can acquire bitcoin in several different ways. These include:

• Purchasing it

- Working for it
- Receiving it as a gift
- Mining it
- Winning it (by playing games for sats or getting a sats-back rewards card)

However, for the sake of brevity, we are going to focus on the three primary ways individuals purchase bitcoin:
- Centralized Exchanges
- Decentralized Exchanges & Peer-to-Peer exchanges.
- Bitcoin ATMs

Let's dive in...

Centralized Exchanges

Your standard online exchange is a centralized market operator that makes it easy for people to buy and sell bitcoin. This removes the problem of locating a counterparty to buy from or sell to. Instead, you simply set up an account and interact directly with the exchange through their mobile or desktop software/website.

Most countries and jurisdictions have both bitcoin-specific and crypto exchanges that offer bitcoin.

Exchanges are, by and large, the most common way to purchase bitcoin. Once you create an account, submit the required personal details and jump through the required hoops, you'll be able to deposit fiat currency into the exchange. After the exchange has received your deposit and updated your account balance, you'll be given a myriad of options for purchasing and selling bitcoin.

These options usually include but are not limited to:

- **Market Order** - The ability to buy/sell bitcoin at the current

3 The Various Ways To Interact with Bitcoin

market price.
- **Automatic Recurring Buys** - The ability to pre-set a purchase interval for which to buy bitcoin, i.e. $10 every week on Tuesdays.
  Also known as dollar cost averaging (DCA).
- **Traditional Order Types** - Order types, such as limit orders, stop
  orders, good-till-date, good-till-cancelled etc., give you much
  greater control. For instance, with a limit order, you can predefine
  a price at which you feel comfortable buying bitcoin. The moment
  this price is hit, the purchase order is automatically triggered.

If you have previously had the privilege of investing in the stock
markets, you should be familiar with these concepts, as you would go
through a similar process to buy a share in a company.
Any entity operating as an investment and financial services company
(facilitating the exchange of bitcoin) must follow certain rules. With
centralized exchanges falling under this category, they must follow
KYC (Know-Your-Customer) and AML (Anti-Money-Laundering) regulations. In addition, regulated exchanges must comply by providing
the governments, tax agencies or regulatory bodies with your personal
details and the information surrounding your bitcoin purchases.

Decentralized Exchanges & Peer-to-Peer exchanges
A decentralized exchange connects two parties, a buyer and seller,
looking to exchange bitcoin. They remove the challenge of inde-
pendently locating a local counterparty with which to transact.

One way to think about peer-to-peer exchanges is simply a Craiglist of
sorts for Bitcoin. A place to find people looking to buy and sell bitcoin.

Once two counterparties connect with one another and coordinate the
specifics of the transaction, these exchanges serve as intermediaries
through the use of smart contracts. The buyer and seller send their
money or bitcoin to a specified holding account (An escrow account).
The exchange then releases the funds once both parties have met the

terms of the trade.

Decentralized exchanges, being relatively new, are in somewhat of a grey zone regarding regulation. Therefore, some comply with KYC and AML practices, while others may not.

Why use a peer-to-peer exchange? As there is no intermediary, peer-to-peer exchanges often allow users to bypass the KYC/AML regulations. If you are privacy-focused or prefer to interact with individuals rather than exchanges, p2p exchanges are a great option.

We highly recommend you become familiar with the rules and regulations in your jurisdiction and transact with bitcoin before exploring decentralized and p2p exchanges, as they are not without risk.

Bitcoin ATMs
Similar to a traditional ATM, the only difference is that you input cash, a debit or credit card, select the amount you wish to purchase, and the machine gives you bitcoin in return.

Some ATMs will provide a paper receipt with a public and private key. Others allow you to send the bitcoin directly to a wallet via a QR code. While most Bitcoin ATMs only allow users to purchase bitcoin, some more sophisticated ones let users both buy and sell it safely and securely.

Bitcoin ATMs can be found in many locations around the globe, but in many countries, they are still hard to come by. There tend to be higher concentrations in cities and areas that are Bitcoin-friendly.

Since centralized businesses usually own these Bitcoin ATMs, most of the time, they must follow the KYC and AML practices mentioned above. In saying that, if you're lucky, you may stumble across some of the earlier ATMs that allow you to purchase Bitcoin without entering personal details—a sought-after commodity in the Bitcoin world.

...and those are the three primary ways to purchase bitcoin.

Section Summary

Like running a node, the decision on where to purchase bitcoin is up to you, your needs and what is available in your jurisdiction.

However, as should be evident, every purchasing method has draw-backs. For this reason, we hope this section has laid out the advantages and disadvantages of each method so you can make a more informed decision, minimize any potential for loss, and reduce any unnecessary headaches.

Now that we understand the various ways to purchase bitcoin, let's move on and look at how we can safely and securely store our bitcoin.

SECTION 6

Custody

Key Questions Answered:
What is a digital wallet?
What is a custodian?
What is self-custody?
How do I back up my seed phrase?
What are the primary solutions for self-custody?
What are hybrid custody solutions?

> **Side Note:** The goal here is not to be an all-encompassing breakdown of existing offerings on the market but rather an attempt to offer a high-level overview of the various forms of custody, alongside their advantages and disadvantages.

Throughout your time exploring the Bitcoin community, you have probably heard the term "custody" or the often-used saying, "Not your keys, not your coins." This section is about understanding what it means to take custody of your bitcoin, and more importantly, what options are available and the trade-offs between them.

To start, let's define some terms:

Custody

The word custody quite literally means "the protective care or guard-ianship of someone or something." In the world of bitcoin, when we talk about custody, we are referring to how we take possession of our bitcoin.

"Shall I use a custodian to look after my bitcoin?"
"Shall I take ownership myself?"
"Or would it be best for me to use some form of a hybrid solution?"
These are all questions surrounding custody.

Wallet

Although a digital wallet, in practice, is similar to a traditional wallet like the one in your pocket, in actuality, they are quite different. A physical wallet stores coins and notes/bills, while a digital "wallet" does not store bitcoin. Instead, it holds the private key that gives access to your bitcoin.

A physical wallet can quickly become quite cumbersome once you have a handful of coins and a dozen notes/bills. On the other hand, a digital wallet storing one satoshi will be no different in size from one holding 21 million satoshis.

Like most technologies, there is usually a myriad of solutions, all with various benefits and trade-offs. It is, therefore, important to under-stand these trade-offs to make a more informed decision on which solution best meets your goals.

When examining any custody solution, we must evaluate how it per-forms in each of these five categories:

1. **Security** - How safe, secure, and up-to-date with industry-standard security practices is this custody solution?
2. **Convenience** - How easy is it to access your bitcoin?
3. **Ease of use** - How easy is the custody solution to operate?
4. **Privacy** - How privacy-focused is this custody solution?
5. **Risks** - What are the primary risks surrounding this custody solution?

> **Side Note:** Before purchasing bitcoin, we highly recommend researching which custody solution works best for you and your specific situation.

In general, there are three types of custody solutions:

- **Custodians** (Someone else controls your private key) - These solutions require putting trust in a third party. This third party then becomes the bearer of your private key (bitcoin).
- **Self-Custody** (You control your private key) - These solutions put the owner of any bitcoin in charge of looking after their own bitcoin. You are responsible for safeguarding access to your private key because it is not stored anywhere else.
- **Hybrid Solutions** (You control some or all of your private key(s)) - These solutions use a mixture of custodians and self-custody to store bitcoin.

Let's explore each of these solutions in more depth:

Custodians - Someone else controls your private key

How do you know whether your wallet is custodial or self-custodial?

When setting up a new wallet, if it asks you to write down a 12 - 24 word seed phrase. Or, when you go to the app security settings, you have access to your seed phrase or private key, then you are taking self-custody of your bitcoin.

If you cannot locate your seed phrase or private key, you are most likely using a custodial wallet.

Exchange Wallets & Centralized Apps

For most people, you will more than likely have purchased your bitcoin through an exchange. Therefore, a custodian is likely the first wallet you'll ever interact with, and the wallet type most people will be familiar with, whether they are aware of it or not.

When you first purchase bitcoin through an exchange, the exchange/ app creates a bitcoin wallet for you. Although you pulled the trigger on buying the bitcoin, while your bitcoin is left on the exchange, they are the custodian.

The problem with this is that, in essence, you do not hold your bitcoin. You have an IOU for your bitcoin. This is where the term "Not your keys, not your coins." comes from. If you do not hold the private key/ seed phrase to your bitcoin, say goodbye to your bitcoin if the exchange becomes insolvent.

How does the exchange store its customer's bitcoin? More often than not, they manage their customer's account balances through a backend central ledger which indicates who owns what. This is similar to the ledger of a bank.

When you buy bitcoin on an exchange or centralized app, it is most likely an off-chain transaction. Although the user experience gives you the impression that you have your own unique bitcoin wallet, in reality, the exchange has a few master wallets containing all of its customers' funds, and your account balance is simply what is indicated on the backend ledger.

This benefits the exchange and the users in two ways:
Reduces transaction fees
Removes the hassle of managing the private keys of every one of their customers

These master wallets can be seen when you send bitcoin to your exchange wallet and locate the transaction on mempool.space. You'll notice that the bitcoin is usually sent to a large exchange wallet, often containing a lot more bitcoin than would be in your account.

Moving on, let's look at the five categories listed above:

Security
With an exchange, you are at the mercy of the exchange's security practices, as well as your own security measures, i.e. the safe keeping of your login information.

Questions to explore when it comes to exchanges:
- Is the exchange a well-known and trusted exchange?
- Do they follow standard industry security practices and provide details on managing their private keys/funds?
- Has the exchange been previously hacked?
- Do they have 1:1 bitcoin holdings to claims? In other words, they do not rehypothecate (create more bitcoin than they have in reserves)

Ease of Use
An exchange wallet is often considered easier to use than other custody solutions because you don't have to manage your private key. To access your bitcoin, you just need your login details and any Two-Factor-Authentication information (which we HIGHLY recommend you

enable).

Convenience
Most exchanges offer both desktop and mobile applications. This means your bitcoin is often at your fingertips when you need it.

Privacy
Exchanges can see your personal information, transactions and balances held within your account. These details can, therefore, be forwarded to government agencies upon their request/demand. Why? As mentioned previously, exchanges must follow KYC (Know-Your-Customer) and AML (Anti-Money-Laundering) regulations.

Risks
The significant risks associated with exchanges usually include forgotten passwords, exchange hacks, exchange private key mismanagement, loss of privacy, malware/phishing attacks etc.

In 2022 alone, we saw three major exchanges declare bankruptcy, FTX, Celsius and Voyager. In all three situations, many customers lost their life savings through no fault of their own other than putting faith in the exchange. This, therefore, brings us to self-custody solutions.

Self-Custody - You control your private key

RECOMMENDED!

As mentioned above, self-custody signifies you are the one in possession of your bitcoin because you control the private key. You, therefore, take on the responsibility of safeguarding your private key because it is not stored anywhere else.

This is what it means when you hear, "Bitcoin allows you to be your own bank." Through self-custody, you are the only one who can access your bitcoin. Although this is the logical next step after using a custodian and removing any third-party risk, that doesn't mean there aren't risks involved with self-custody.

When it comes to self-custody, securely storing your private key is of the utmost importance. If someone gains access to your private key, they have control of your bitcoin. That said, before diving into the self-custody solutions, let's first go over the very important step of how to back up your seed phrase.

Seed-phrase Backups.

Backing up your seed phrase is a vital step in the journey of taking self-custody of your bitcoin. Learning effective seed-phrase backup practices is imperative to eliminate single points of failure.

When you set up a self-custody wallet, you are given your 12 or 24-word seed phrase. Write down your seed phrase on a piece of paper (usually provided). Once you have confirmed that you've correctly recorded your seed phrase, you can proceed to send funds to the wallet.

However, your work is not done...

You need to secure that backup properly.

There are several ways you can do this[42]. For instance, etching your seed phrase into steel will give your wealth an extra layer of protection from fire and flood. A quick google search will assist you in finding a solution that works best for you.

And finally, once you have securely backed up your seed phrase, it is vitally important that it is kept secure or hidden, such as in a safe or locked filing cabinet.

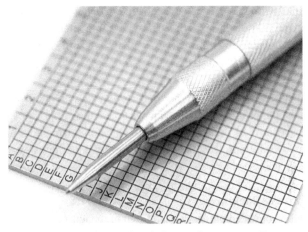

Figure 3.51: Metal Seed Plate Made By CoinKite[43]

Why is seed phrase backup and storage so important?

Quite simply, with great power comes great responsibility. Taking part in a decentralized financial ecosystem with no intermediaries comes with one major shortfall. There is no "undo" button when it comes to transactions, and there is no help desk to call when you can't find your seed phrase.

If your hardware wallet is damaged, lost or stolen, and you forgot to backup your seed phrase, your assets are gone.

Side note: It is important to physically record this phrase. Never make a digital copy of your seed phrase, i.e. phone notes, online, or through a screenshot/picture. If you do and someone hacks your digital device, they will have access to your bitcoin.

Back to self-custody...

Primary Solutions for Self-Custody

Let's take a look at the three primary solutions for self-custody:

- **Cold Wallet** - Often referred to as "cold storage," cold wallets are a way of storing bitcoin in an offline hardware device. By storing your bitcoin in an offline device, such as a Cold Card, Ledger or Trezor, investors reduce the risk of hackers accessing their holdings through conventional channels, such as exchanges that are at times vulnerable to attack.
- **Hot Wallets** - The "hot" part of the term "hot wallet" refers to the fact that these wallets are on a desktop or mobile connected to the internet. Because they are connected to the internet, they have a greater risk of being hacked over a cold wallet. Therefore, while a hot wallet is often superior to a cold wallet in terms of ease of use and convenience, it is not deemed the most secure option for taking custody of your bitcoin.
- **Brain Wallets** - With a brain wallet, another form of cold storage, you store your bitcoin by memorizing your private key as a seed phrase. We do not advise this method because of the ease of forgetting your seed phrase and thereby losing your bitcoin. A brain wallet should be your last-ditch option for storing your bitcoin in emergencies, i.e. fleeing a war-torn country.

Let's now look at how self-custody performs in the five categories listed above:

Security

You are no longer at the mercy of the exchange's security practices with self-custody. However, you take full responsibility for storing your private key/seed phrase. This poses its own issues, but generally, as long as you take good care of your seed phrase and store it securely, you remove any third-party risks, such as those experienced through an exchange. In saying that, hot wallets generally have greater exposure to hacks and security threats due to being located on a mobile device or desktop computer.

Ease of Use
Technology is rapidly improving, with the user experience of many self-custody solutions today indistinguishable from their centralized exchange counterpart. However, in terms of ease of use, hot wallets on your phone or desktop tend to be easier to use than their cold storage siblings. However, there is an increased security risk in return for this ease of use.

Convenience
Similar to ease of use, hot wallets allow users to quickly and easily transfer funds and perform daily transactions, albeit with slightly reduced security over their cold wallet sibling. Cold wallets, on the other hand, although relatively easy to use, are usually more time-consuming, given that you have to locate your hardware device to sign and validate the transaction.

Depending on the cold storage hardware wallet, some manufacturers will provide proprietary software to manage your bitcoin. Others allow you to use their software or a software wallet of your choice.

Privacy
Self-custody solutions are, by and large, the best way to ensure privacy when transacting. Because of their "be your own bank" nature, they are permissionless. You are not passing over personal information to a third-party or requesting access from someone else to move your bitcoin.

Risks
The major risks associated with self-custody solutions revolve around forgetting or losing your private key/seed phrase or malware/phishing

attacks.

Figure 3.52: *Examples of Various Hardware Wallets*[44]

Hybrid & Alternative Solutions - You control some or all of your private key(s)

These solutions usually require a mix of self-custodial and custodial solutions.

Let's explore the most common alternate solution, multi-signature wallets.

Multi-signature a.k.a Multi-sig

One of the primary issues with the self-custody solutions listed above is that you have a single point of failure. If someone locates your seed phrase, they have access to your funds. One way to eliminate this is to use what is known as a multi-signature wallet.

A multi-sig wallet secures your bitcoin behind multiple private keys, whereby a pre-set combination of these keys gains you access to your bitcoin, i.e. two-of-three, three-of-five, five-of-eight etc. These different variations symbolize how many keys out of the total amount of keys are needed to sign the transaction. For instance, in a three-of-five set-up, any three out of the five keys can be used to sign a transaction.

What makes multi-signature wallets so secure is that there are endless possibilities for storing these private keys, e.g., you could geographically disburse each key so that no one location houses all the necessary private keys to access your funds. Alternatively, you could share each key with a friend or family member so that to them, each key is worthless, but combined, you still have access to your funds. Or, for inheritance planning, you could leave one of the keys with a lawyer.

Why take all the trouble to disperse your keys? Let's say you have a two of three multi-signature setup, and someone locates one of your private keys, or in the example above, your trusted friend or family member turns on you. Even though they have access to one of your private keys, there is no way for them to access your bitcoin unless they manage to obtain the pre-set amount of private keys, i.e. two out of three, three out of five etc. A much harder task.

Why are multi-sig wallets sometimes classified as a hybrid solution? How you store your keys will dictate whether your multi-sig wallet falls under hybrid or self-custody. If you control all your private keys, this would be classified as a self-custody solution.

However, if you store one or more of your private keys with custodians, although there is no single point of failure, you're inviting a third party into your custody solution. It would, therefore, be considered a hybrid solution.

As there are many variations to multi-signature and hybrid wallets, all with varying advantages and disadvantages, we won't explore the security, ease of use, convenience, privacy and risks we have with the other options.

However, we will say that if you are looking to store your bitcoin long-term and want to minimize single points of failure, a geographically dispersed multi-sig approach is one of the safest options. That said, with current technology, setting up a multi-sig solution requires an understanding of best practices and technical knowledge, so it is best to seek guidance during your initial setup.

Section Summary

Tying up chapter three, it can be easy at first to see bitcoin as this thing that you buy and sell. However, as we have explored, there is so much more to it than this.

Whether you're interested in mining bitcoin, getting involved in consensus, monitoring blockchain activity, taking self-custody, or experimenting with both on-chain and off-chain transactions, Bitcoin caters to everybody.

That said, no matter where your interests lie, we all have to decide how to custody our Bitcoin. You may, therefore, be wondering, "what custody solution is best for me?"

Unfortunately, as this article has shown, there is no single answer to this question.

How you take custody is unique to you, your technical know-how and the amount being custodied.

We highly recommend people to self-custody, but we also recognize that for some, self-custody is not a viable option. With this in mind, here are some general guidelines:

Exchanges are great for purchasing bitcoin, hot wallets are great for everyday transactions, and cold or multi-sig wallets are ideal for storing your long-term bitcoin savings.

Consider a hot wallet the same way you consider your physical wallet, and only keep as much bitcoin in it as you would in your regular wallet.

You can think of your cold wallet or multi-sig setup as your savings account– money that doesn't require frequent access, and its long-term safety and security are the priority.

If you're exploring what self-custody solutions may be best for you, we highly recommend checking out Ben from BTCsessions[45] on YouTube.

In the final chapter, we will go through a fictional example of the life-cycle of a bitcoin and then conclude with our final remarks.

See you in the last chapter.

CHAPTER 4

The Lifecycle of a bitcoin

"Once a new technology rolls over you, if you're not part of the steamroller, you're part of the road." - Stewart Brand

SECTION 1

Bitcoin in Action

Key Questions Answered:
What are some examples of Bitcoin in action?

To wrap things up, we will explore the hypothetical lifecycle of a bitcoin, following the journey of a newly-minted bitcoin from birth to cold storage and everything in between. This scenario will help cement some of the terms and learnings we have covered and give you a better understanding of Bitcoin, the network and bitcoin, the asset.

The Birth of New Bitcoin

If you recall from our example in "On-chain & Off-chain," we introduced Dan and Josh. Two avid Bitcoiners. What we didn't mention was that Dan and Josh are so enamoured by Bitcoin that they decided to set up a mining company. Based out of Texas, this mining company focuses on portable mining rigs and partners with oil companies to reduce methane and C02 emissions[46] by capturing flared methane and using the heat to generate power for their miners.

With their miners successfully up and running in the first week of operation, they triumphantly mine their first Bitcoin block, #753,835[47]. This block contains 6.25 BTC of virgin bitcoin + 0.155 BTC in transaction fees for a total block reward of 6.405 bitcoin. This bitcoin is immediately sent to the company's self-custody address, which they included within the block information they broadcasted to the network.

Although Dan and Josh are thrilled about mining their first block, they laugh, wishing they had started this mining operation during the last Bitcoin halving. If they had, the same block would have contained 12.5 virgin bitcoin rather than 6.25. But Dan and Josh are still excited about what the future holds. And they are motivated to mine as many blocks as possible before the next halving in 2024.

On-Chain & Multi-Signature

With Dan and Josh operating a Bitcoin mining company out of Texas, their expenses are denominated in US dollars (USD). Therefore, at the end of the first month, they total their expenses, which come to $73,200. With Dan and Josh having used all their USD to start the mining operation, they need to convert some of their bitcoin proceeds into USD.

Dan and Josh use a two-of-three multi-signature wallet, with Dan securely storing one private key, Josh another, and their silent partner with the final key. This means Dan and Josh combined have two of the three private keys and can, therefore, sign transactions on behalf of their mining company.

With this in mind, they set up an account with a local centralized bitcoin exchange, create a transaction to send BTC to their exchange address and sign the transaction with Dan and Josh's two cold-storage devices.

This signed transaction is now broadcast from their software wallet to the network, sending 3.26 bitcoin (~$73,200 at the exchange rate on the day) on-chain from their company's treasury to their exchange account.

As Dan and Josh run their own node, not only are they involved in consensus for Bitcoin improvements, they can view the status of the transaction before their balance is visible on the exchange.

They, therefore, log into the backend of their node to view mempool. space privately, paste their transaction ID and see that the network has confirmed their transaction. They can also see that it cost them 7,131 sats (approximately $1.50 at the time) to send the 3.26 BTC. This leaves them with a balance of 3.14492869 bitcoin in their self-custody wallet.

Once the bitcoin arrives in Dan and Josh's centralized exchange account, they immediately convert it to USD.

Dan and Josh's account now displays a balance of $73,200 USD, and the exchange receives the recently deposited 3.26 bitcoin. After the conversion is complete, they transfer this USD balance into their linked business bank account and pay their bills.

Importance of Self-Custody

With the 3.26 bitcoin in the exchange's reserves, it is now available for purchase from other customers using that exchange. Within a few days, two customers, Dane and Sally, decide to buy some bitcoin and become the new owners of this bitcoin.

Sally decided to invest her hard-earned savings, purchasing 0.25 BTC, while Dane invested a portion of his monthly income by purchasing 0.02 bitcoin. However, both take a slightly different approach to securing their newly purchased bitcoin.

Dane

With limited knowledge of third-party custody risks, Dane is of the buy-it-and-forget-it mindset. Once purchased, he leaves his bitcoin on the exchange.

As safe as it initially seemed, unfortunately for Dane, the exchange finds itself in financial trouble. It had been lending out customers' deposits to secure some extra income. After one too many defaults on these loans, its customers caught on and started withdrawing their bitcoin. Initially unaware, Dane eventually contacts the exchange. But by this point, they have stopped allowing customer withdrawals. The exchange eventually declares itself bankrupt, and Dane loses his bitcoin.

Dane's example illustrates the importance of self-custody. In his case, he had third-party exposure by leaving his bitcoin on the exchange.

"Not your keys, not your coins."

Sally

Sally is a long-term bitcoiner that deeply understands the risks of storing her hard-earned bitcoin on the exchange.

She, therefore, quickly withdraws her bitcoin from the exchange, removing any custodial risk. She sends 0.22 BTC to her secure, self-custody cold storage and 0.03 BTC to her mobile hot wallet in two separate on-chain transactions.

Off-chain

In the coming weeks, Sally and her best friend Rosa will head to El Salvador to visit Bitcoin Beach. Sally's initial thought is that as merchants in El Salvador accept bitcoin through the Lightning network, she could use her hot wallet to transact with them.

Sally loves the idea of supporting local vendors with bitcoin. Not only does it reduce the merchant fees on the vendor's end, but it also eliminates her foreign exchange rates and exorbitant international ATM withdrawal fees.

Figure 4.11: El Zonte a.k.a Bitcoin Beach[48]

When Sally arrives in El Salvador, the first thing she does is convert her hot wallet bitcoin balance into Lightning. Through this off-chain technology, she can quickly and anonymously transact with merchants for fractions of a cent.

Seed Phrase Back-Up

Initially, Sally's friend Rosa doesn't know much about Bitcoin, although she quickly recognizes its versatility after watching Sally

4 The Lifecycle of a bitcoin

interact with the local vendors.

As Rosa purchased lunch during the first few days, Sally suggested that she pay Rosa back via bitcoin. Rosa is intrigued. She downloads a hot wallet app on her phone, creates a new wallet and is ready to go. Rosa hits receive via lightning which presents a QR code, Sally scans the QR using her hot wallet app, and Sally sends Rosa 200,000 satoshis for a total fee of 99 sats or $0.02.

After the transaction is complete, Sally stresses to Rosa the importance of backing up her wallet when they return to the hotel that night to ensure she can always access her bitcoin balance no matter what may happen to her phone.

When they return to the hotel, Rosa takes note of her seed phrase. After securely recording her seed phrase, Rosa chooses to top up her wallet with some more funds, so she heads down to a bitcoin ATM in the lobby. Rosa uses her credit card in the ATM and transfers an additional equivalent of $200 worth of bitcoin into her wallet. She scans the QR code with her hot wallet app, and in an instant, 898,836 satoshis arrive in her wallet, giving her a total balance of 1,098,836 sats.

Merchants

That night, Sally and Rosa head out and enjoy an amazing dinner and drinks at a local Argentine restaurant. When it comes time to pay the bill, Juan, the restaurant owner, quickly and effortlessly displays bitcoin and lightning payment options through his Bitcoin-integrated Point-Of-Sale (POS) system. Rosa chooses Lightning and pays the bill for 119,992 sats. Within a few seconds, they're ready to go.

As Sally and Rosa leave, Rosa asks Juan about using Bitcoin as a business. Juan's face lights up as he explains, "Not only do I save the 2-6% transaction fee when it comes to processing traditional payment methods, but the transactions using Lightning are instantaneous, and I can obtain final settlement. Credit card payments, on the other hand, usually take 2-4 days for transactions to settle (he has to wait before he obtains access to these funds). During this time, there is the possibility for transactions to be reversed. That is not the case with Bitcoin's final settlement." Juan ends with the fact that he's been converted and fully supports merchant Bitcoin adoption.

Remittance

After Rosa and Sally leave, Juan closes up shop for the night. However, just before Juan heads home, he remembers his daughter back in Argentina, Isabella. It's her birthday. He wants to surprise her with money for her savings. Traditionally, Juan would send money through Western Union and incur fees upwards of 20%[49]. However, since adopting Bitcoin, the process has been much cheaper and easier.

Juan calls Isabella. She opens her hot wallet app and creates a Lightning invoice which she sends over Whatsapp to her dad. He copies and pastes it into his wallet, adding the amount he wishes to send, and within an instant, 496,034 satoshis ($100) arrive in Isabella's wallet for a cost of 87 sats ($0.01). No intermediaries, no permission needed and all for a fraction of the cost of traditional money transfers.

Cold Storage

Isabella having spent the last few years studying the history of Argentina, is all too familiar with the fact that the government has defaulted on their debt obligations nine times[50] in the previous 200 years. But, more importantly, she has lost confidence in storing her savings in the local currency with their rampant annualized inflation of 191% from

1944 - 2022[51].

Isabella, therefore, opts to store her savings in bitcoin, knowing that her 0.1 bitcoin of 21,000,000 today will still be 0.1 of 21,000,000 in ten years. Isabella takes a long-term view of her savings. The short-term volatility does not worry her too much. In fact, she likes it when bitcoin's price falls in USD terms as she can purchase more bitcoin for the same amount of money.

Isabella also feels comfortable knowing there is no way for a centralized body to dilute the currency by expanding the money supply. On the other hand, Argentina[52], which had 200 billion pesos in circulation in 2012, now (August of 2022) has 3.234 trillion. A 1,512% increase over the last ten years. Putting that in perspective, if Juan had sent $100 worth of pesos rather than bitcoin to Isabella in 2012, she could only purchase $3 worth of goods today. A 97%[53] reduction in purchasing power.

Knowing this, Isabella opens up her hot wallet and converts her off-chain lightning balance into bitcoin. She then creates a new transaction, enters her cold storage wallet address and sends over her balance of 0.00496034 BTC. Isabella then sighs with a sense of relief, knowing that she has minimized any third-party risks, with her bitcoin tucked away in cold storage as she heads off to bed. That night she dreams of all the things that her bitcoin may purchase in the future. She also imagines what a "hyperbitcoinized[54]" world may look like where people can be their own bank and trust that governments and central banks will not devalue their money through money printing.

Section Summary

With only one section left, the final conclusion, we just want to say a preemptive thank you for taking the time to read this book and joining us on this journey.

Hopefully, through this little fictional story, you can see how Bitcoin, the asset and the network work in conjunction with one another. But more importantly, how various individuals with different ideals and needs use bitcoin.

In this story, we followed some bitcoin from mining to entering the bitcoin circular economy, to being spent and then handed over from user to user until they reached their slumber in Isabella's cold storage, hopefully assisting her in building generational wealth. However, this is but one example of the path bitcoin might take, and we have only just scratched the surface of some of the many use cases bitcoin has to offer.

As you continue your Bitcoin journey, you'll encounter many stories like this, the only difference being that they will be real.

If you come across any extraordinary stories, be sure to share them with us.

Conclusion

Congratulations on making it to the end. We hope you have enjoyed this journey through the world of Bitcoin.

We have taken you along the journey that we, the authors, and many others, have been on in our quest to truly understand the ins and outs of this incredible nascent technology.

Typically, it takes hundreds if not thousands of hours to trawl through the plethora of phenomenal resources (books, podcasts and YouTube tutorials) explaining how Bitcoin works and why it is one of the fastest-growing assets in history.

What we have attempted to do throughout this book is to distill those 1000 hours of learning into a one-stop learning solution. Our goal was to take the reader through Bitcoin's inception and mysterious past. All while exploring the players, the protocol and the facts and figures that make Bitcoin the fully functioning and resilient asset it is today.

We hope we have achieved this and you have gained some helpful insights and learnings. We would love to hear your thoughts and feedback, so do not hesitate to reach out.

If you enjoyed this book, the best thing you can do is to share it amongst your friends and family and on your favourite social media platforms.

Lastly, we intend to keep as many of our educational resources free and available to budding bitcoiners everywhere! We, therefore, greatly appreciate any donations to help us create even more educational material for those who need this most.
Thank you for entrusting us with your learning experience and we

hope to have even more content to share with you in the near future.

Sincerely,

The Looking Glass Team

The future is bright!

Bibliography

1. "Senator Elizabeth Warren Says Crypto Puts Financial System at Mercy of 'Faceless Super Coders.'" The Daily Hodl, 29 July 2021, https://dailyhodl.com/2021/07/29/senator-elizabeth-warren-says-crypto-puts-financial-system-at-mercy-of-faceless-super-coders/. Accessed 5 February 2023.

2. Nakamoto, Satoshi. "A Peer-to-Peer Electronic Cash System." Bitcoin.org, https://bitcoin.org/bitcoin.pdf. Accessed 5 February 2023.

3. Diffie, Whitfield, and Martin Hellman. "Cypherpunk." Wikipedia, https://en.wikipedia.org/wiki/Cypherpunk. Accessed 5 February 2023.

4. Bach, Adam. "Adam Back on Satoshi Emails, Privacy Concerns and Bitcoin's Early Days." Cointelegraph, 20 January 2020, https://cointelegraph.com/news/adam-back-on-satoshi-emails-privacy-concerns-and-bitcoins-early-days. Accessed 5 February 2023.

5. "What Was the First Cryptocurrency?" Investopedia, https://www.investopedia.com/tech/were-there-cryptocurrencies-bitcoin/. Accessed 5 February 2023.

6. "Gmail - Holding coins in an unspendable state for a rolling time window." Mike Hearn, 18 April 2011, https://plan99.net/~mike/satoshi-emails/thread5.html. Accessed 5 February 2023.

7. Nakamoto, Satoshi. "Bitcoin open source implementation of P2P currency – P2P Foundation." P2P Foundation, 11 February 2009, http://p2pfoundation.ning.com/forum/topics/bitcoin-open-source?commentId=2003008%3AComment%3A52186. Accessed 5 February 2023.

8. Rasure, Erika. "3 People Who Were Supposedly Bitcoin Founder Satoshi Nakamoto." Investopedia, https://www.investopedia.com/tech/three-people-who-were-supposedly-bitcoin-founder-sa-

toshi-nakamoto/. Accessed 5 February 2023.

9. "Visa, Mastercard Move To Choke Wikileaks." YouTube, 10 August 2022, https://www.forbes.com/sites/andy-greenberg/2010/12/07/visa-mastercard-move-to-choke-wikileaks/?sh=614d78052cad. Accessed 5 February 2023.

10. Rabiner, Stephanie. "Make Your Own Currency, Spend 5 Years in Jail." FindLaw, 23 January 2012, https://www.findlaw.com/legalblogs/legally-weird/make-your-own-currency-spend-5-years-in-jail/. Accessed 5 February 2023.

11. Duncan, Gary. "Chancellor Alistair Darling on brink of second bailout for banks." The Times, 3 January 2009, https://www.the-times.co.uk/article/chancellor-alistair-darling-on-brink-of-second-bailout-for-banks-n9l382mn62h. Accessed 5 February 2023.

12. Napier, Patricia. "Royal Protocol Briefing." Etiquette School of New York, https://etiquette-ny.com/royal-protocol-briefing/. Accessed 5 February 2023.

13. Pantera Capital. "The Money over Internet Protocol." Wikipedia, Pantera, 2015, https://us3.campaign-archive.com/?u=e99fe-22821ab514a67a0aae2e&id=e77c72aa46. Accessed 8 March 2023.

14. "Neel Kashkari unlimited Fed printing." YouTube, 23 March 2020, https://www.youtube.com/watch?v=DUrlNHTxuJM. Accessed 5 February 2023.

15. "What is Decentralization?" AWS, https://aws.amazon.com/blockchain/decentralization-in-blockchain/. Accessed 5 February 2023.

16. Benjamin, Godfrey. "Blockchain vs Distributed Ledger Technology (DLT) Differences." iMi Blockchain, 22 May 2021, https://imiblockchain.com/blockchain-vs-distributed-ledger-technology/. Accessed 8 March 2023.

17. Bitnodes: Reachable Bitcoin Nodes, https://bitnodes.io/. Accessed 5 February 2023.

18. "Global Bitcoin Nodes." Bitnodes, https://bitnodes.io/nodes/all/. Accessed 5 February 2023.

19. SHA256 Online, https://emn178.github.io/online-tools/sha256. html. Accessed 5 February 2023.

20. "The Bitcoin Standard Podcast: 114. Why Bitcoin Changes Accounting with Darin Feinstein on Apple Podcasts." Apple Podcasts, https://podcasts.apple.com/us/podcast/114-why-bitcoin-changes-accounting-with-darin-feinstein/id1403202032?i=1000560789476. Accessed 5 February 2023.

21. Rasure, Erika. "Genesis Block: Bitcoin Definition, Mysteries, Secret Message." Investopedia, https://www.investopedia.com/terms/g/genesis-block.asp. Accessed 5 February 2023.

22. "Transaction: 4a5e1e4baab89f3a32518a88c31bc87f-618f76673e2cc77ab2127b7afdeda33b - mempool - Bitcoin Explorer." Mempool, https://mempool.space/tx/4a5e1e4baab-89f3a32518a88c31bc87f618f76673e2cc77ab2127b7afdeda33b. Accessed 5 February 2023.

23. Back, Adam. A Primer On Bitcoin Mining, https://assets-global. website-files.com/614e11536f66309636c98688/626c1a0d-3ba033b7326745e9_A%20Primer%20On%20Bitcoin%20Mining-Small.pdf. Accessed 5 February 2023.

24. "Next Bitcoin Halving 2024 Date & Countdown [BTC Clock]." Buy Bitcoin Worldwide, https://www.buybitcoinworldwide.com/bitcoin-clock/. Accessed 5 February 2023.

25. "Debt, Inflation & the Bigger Picture Course - The Looking Glass." The Looking Glass Education, https://lookingglasseducation.com/courses/free-foundation-course/. Accessed 5 February 2023.

26. Cipolaro, Greg, and Ethan Kochav. "A Primer On Bitcoin Mining." NYDIG, 29 April 2022, https://nydig.com/research/a-primer-on-bitcoin-mining. Accessed 8 March 2023.

27. "How secure is 256 bit security?" YouTube, 10 August 2022, https://www.youtube.com/watch?v=S9JGmA5_unY&t=191s. Accessed 5 February 2023.

28. "Home BIP39 Word List." Privacy Pros, https://privacypros.io/bip39-word-list/. Accessed 5 February 2023.

29. "Bitcoin: Total Addresses." Glassnode Studio, https://studio.

glassnode.com/metrics?a=BTC&category=Addresses&m=addresses.Count. Accessed 5 February 2023.

30. Glassnode - On-chain market intelligence, https://glassnode.com/. Accessed 5 February 2023.

31. Wyland, Lucas, and Mitchell Cookson. "The 10 Best Bitcoin Mining Hardware Machines 2023." CoinLedger, https://coinledger.io/tools/best-bitcoin-mining-hardware. Accessed 5 February 2023.

32. Back, Adam. A Primer On Bitcoin Mining, https://assets-global.website-files.com/614e11536f66309636c98688/626c1a0d-3ba033b7326745e9_A%20Primer%20On%20Bitcoin%20Mining-Small.pdf. Accessed 5 February 2023.

33. "Bitcoin Hashrate Chart." BitInfoCharts, https://bitinfocharts.com/comparison/bitcoin-hashrate.html. Accessed 5 February 2023.

34. "Bitcoin Mining Centralization." YouTube, 10 August 2022, https://www.forbes.com/sites/ktorpey/2019/07/28/bitcoin-mining-centralization-is-quite-alarming-but-a-solution-is-in-the-works/?sh=1ecb4f01530b. Accessed 5 February 2023.

35. "Cambridge Bitcoin Electricity Consumption Index (CBECI)." Cambridge Bitcoin Electricity Consumption Index (CBECI), https://ccaf.io/cbeci/mining_map. Accessed 5 February 2023.

36. "Bitcoin Core." Bitcoin.org, https://bitcoin.org/en/bitcoin-core/. Accessed 5 February 2023.

37. "The Machine with Umbrel - Run your personal Bitcoin and Lightning Node %Bitcoin Node %Bitcoin." The Bitcoin Machine, https://thebitcoinmachines.com/product/machine-with-umbrel/. Accessed 5 February 2023.

38. Bitcoin Guides, https://armantheparman.com/. Accessed 5 February 2023.

39. "bitcoin/bips: Bitcoin Improvement Proposals." GitHub, https://github.com/bitcoin/bips. Accessed 5 February 2023.

40. "The Blockchain Scalability Problem & the Race for Visa-Like Transaction Speed." Towards Data Science, 30 January 2019, https://towardsdatascience.com/the-blockchain-scalability-

problem-the-race-for-visa-like-transaction-speed-5cce48f9d44.
Accessed 5 February 2023.

41. Chandler, Simon. "The 5 Biggest Bitcoin Transactions In History."
CryptoVantage.com, 22 August 2022, https://www.cryptovan-
tage.com/news/here-are-the-5-biggest-bitcoin-transactions-in-his-
tory/. Accessed 5 February 2023.

42. "4 Best Ways To Securely Store Seed Phrase In 2023." CoinSutra,
16 December 2022, https://coinsutra.com/keep-recovery-seed-
safe-secure/. Accessed 5 February 2023.

43. SEEDPLATE™ - Bitcoin Seed Metal Backup, https://seedplate.
com/. Accessed 5 February 2023.

44. Costea, Vlad. "Bitcoin Wallet Reviews: What's the Best Hardware
Wallet on the Market? Part 2." Bitcoin Magazine, 12 November
2019, https://bitcoinmagazine.com/culture/bitcoin-wallet-re-
views-whats-the-best-hardware-wallet-on-the-market-part-2.
Accessed 5 February 2023.

45. Sessions, Ben. "BTCSessions." YouTube, 10 August 2022, https://
www.youtube.com/c/BTCSessions. Accessed 5 February 2023.

46. "How & Why Natural Gas Flaring Is Used To Mine Bitcoin." You-
Tube, 10 August 2022, https://oilmanmagazine.com/how-and-
why-natural-gas-flaring-is-being-used-to-mine-bitcoin/. Accessed
5 February 2023.

47. "Bitcoin Block." YouTube, 10 August 2022, https://mempool.
space/block/0000000000000000000910c46ea1f7d69e4c0c369d-
ce6848ae72b0169f196aea. Accessed 5 February 2023.

48. Salvadorean Tours. "El Zonte El Salvador | Best day tours &
things to do." Salvadorean Tours, 2006, https://salvadoreantours.
com/destination/el-zonte-el-salvador/. Accessed 8 March 2023.

49. "Send Money Worldwide - Money Transfer Service." Western
Union, https://www.westernunion.com/sv/en/send-money.html.
Accessed 5 February 2023.

50. "One Country, Nine Defaults." YouTube, 10 August 2022, https://
www.bloomberg.com/news/photo-essays/2019-09-11/one-coun-
try-eight-defaults-the-argentine-debacles?leadSource=uverify%20

wall. Accessed 5 February 2023.

51. "Argentina Inflation Rate - January 2023 Data - 1944-2022 Historical." Trading Economics, https://tradingeconomics.com/ argentina/inflation-cpi. Accessed 5 February 2023.

52. "Argentina Monetary Base: Currency in Circulation | Economic Indicators." CEIC, https://www.ceicdata.com/en/argentina/ monetary-base/monetary-base-currency-in-circulation. Accessed 5 February 2023.

53. O'Neill, Aaron. "Argentina - inflation rate 2004-2027." Statista, 2 November 2022, https://www.statista.com/statistics/316750/ inflation-rate-in-argentina/. Accessed 5 February 2023.

54. "Hyperbitcoinization Explained." Bitcoin Magazine, https:// bitcoinmagazine.com/hyperbitcoinization. Accessed 5 February 2023.

Made in the USA
Columbia, SC
31 July 2024

39717746R00096